Pursue Love

IT'S YOUR GREATEST NEED
FIRST CORINTHIANS 13

David L. Hocking

Scripture quotations in this book are from the *New American Standard Bible.* © The Lockman Foundation 1960, 1962, 1963, 1968, 1971, 1972, 1973, 1975. Used by permission.
There are also some quotations from the *Authorized King James Version* of the Bible.

Published by Sounds of Grace Publishers
Long Beach, California 90807
Printed in U.S.A.

Graphic design and production by D. Burton Larkey

Library of Congress Catalog Card Number: 80-50393
International Standard Book Number: 0-936642-00-9

Dedication

To my wife, Carole - for the way she loves. My deepest thanks to her for her unselfish devotion to our children, and for the constant encouragement her fervent love and sweet spirit brings to my heart. She is a demonstration to me of the kind of love we all need in our lives. May God continue to bless her for her desire and commitment to love.

Contents

Dr. David L. Hocking, B.A.; M.Div.; D.Min.; Ph.D.
has authored the following publications:

Spiritual Gifts, an extensive manual

Be A Leader People Follow, a book of seven practical
laws on leadership

How To Be Happy In Difficult Situations, a commentary
on the Book of Philippians

The World's Greatest Church, a book of Bible teachings
concerning the Church

Also vest pocket size booklets:

Are The Dead Really Dead?

God's Purpose For Woman!

Let's Be Friends

Israel's Right To The Land!

Who Is Jesus?

Preface

We all have needs, but we are not always aware of which of those needs we should seek to fulfil. Which of our needs are the greatest? Studies continue to show that one of our greatest desires is to be loved. We will do most anything (often what we should not do!) to experience love. Is this great passion to be loved a real need?

The Bible has much to say about our needs and about the importance of love. It seems to suggest (and even command!) that our greatest single need is love. Nothing is more important! Nothing is more needed in our lives! However, the kind of love with which the Bible is concerned, is rarely seen in our lives. It's the only type of love that can ultimately satisfy and bring complete fulfillment to us. Most people remain unaware of how different God's love is from what they are used to experiencing.

One chapter in the Bible says more about love than all the books ever written on that subject. This book is about that chapter. That one chapter can revolutionize your life! It can literally change you and make you to be the kind of person God intended you to be and others admire.

Don't hurry through the principles of this book. Take time to understand and most of all, to apply it to your life. This could be the most important study you have ever made! You may be on the verge of meeting the greatest need in your life!

Pursue **Love**
IT'S YOUR GREATEST NEED
FIRST CORINTHIANS 13

INTRODUCTION

Your greatest need is not money,
fame, success, pleasure, a vacation,
recreation, a better job . . .
Your greatest need is **love!**

Love that only God can give you!
Love, not sentimentality, sex, or
emotional vibrations, but **love!**

Interested?
    Then, read on . . .

The greatest lines ever written on your greatest need are found in the Bible in the thirteenth chapter of the book of I Corinthians. There are 13 verses, 280 words (NASB), and only 3 paragraphs. Not a long dissertation, but what depth! Volumes have been written about *LOVE*, but nothing has been added to the sublime character of these divine words!

This is a view from heaven - it is the correct view about *LOVE* - it is God's view, not man's. Let's face it . . . we've had enough of the opinions and views of man about *LOVE!* It's time for a change! We need to hear from God.

Bathed in the conviction that our greatest need is to know and experience God's *LOVE*, the following pages have been written. They are simple, direct, and practical, but rooted in careful analysis of the text of I Corinthians 13.

I don't know about you, but I need *LOVE* - sometimes I wonder if I'll ever really understand what it is! The Bible speaks of the great dimensions of God's *LOVE* and that it surpasses human comprehension (Ephesians 3:17-19). My mother's favorite song describes the problem of understanding God's *LOVE* - the song is entitled, *"The Love of God."*

> Could we with ink the oceans fill,
> And were the skies of parchment made;
> Were every stalk on earth a quill,
> And every man a scribe by trade;
> To write the **love** of God above
> Would drain the ocean dry.
> Nor could the scroll contain the whole,
> Though stretched from sky to sky.

In trying to understand the teaching of I Corinthians 13 on God's *LOVE*, we must be aware of a few things. *First,* is the "human fallibility factor." We simply do not know as God knows. All we have to go on are His Words. Our ability to understand them is the great variable. But, don't be discouraged . . . there is much we can learn and know about His *LOVE*. Don't be too concerned about what you don't know, but rather what you can and do know! While I am confident that the truth about God's *LOVE* is contained in I

Corinthians 13, I am not so confident that I have interpreted the words correctly. Allow for that, and we can all learn a great deal.

Secondly, we must understand that God wants us to know of His *LOVE* much more than we do. I'm encouraged by that.

Thirdly, remember that God is fully aware of your weaknesses and failures in loving, yet He still loves you! (That should tell you something about His *LOVE!*) Many people give up because of past failures and broken hearts.

Fourthly, His *LOVE* is greater than any human emotion or experience! It's worth your effort to discover it and to experience it!

Fifthly, He will help you to *LOVE* with His *LOVE*, and with divine help, you *can* experience God's *LOVE!* (More about this later!)

I remember the lady who told me she couldn't love anymore. She had been deeply hurt, and all her attempts at loving had been rejected. It's not easy to recover from experiences like that. But, when she grasped the meaning of God's *LOVE*, her confidence began to grow. Before long, she was loving as God intended her to love. What joy can fill our hearts when that happens!

To understand God's *LOVE* we need to evaluate the different words used to express love. The ancient Greeks used at least four different words for love. In English, we use the same word with different meanings. I love ice cream, my dog, and my wife - but there is a big difference in the way I love each of those items! (I'm in trouble if there is no difference!) Let's take a look at the Greek words.

Eros - Physical/sensual love.
It's not used in the Bible, but the concept of sexual love is definitely taught (cf. Song of Solomon). English words like "erotic" come from this Greek word.

Storge - family ties.
It's used of animals as well as people. It refers to the love of a parent for a child.

Phile - psychological/social love.
It's often translated with the word "friend (cf. John 15:13-14)," and is used of God as well as human beings. It's the love of companionship that every marriage must enjoy to survive.
Agape - spiritual/divine love.
It's the love that comes from God (I John 4:7), and is the nature of God Himself (I John 4:8). It's the love described in I Corinthians 13.

The greatest demonstration of "agape" love was at the cross of Jesus Christ (cf. I John 4:9-10; John 3:16). At the heart of this love, is the concept of sacrifice. This love is produced in the lives of believers by the Holy Spirit (Galatians 5:22; Romans 5:5).

Why don't people experience this love in their lives?

Good question . . . and not an easy one to answer! Some Christians can give you a quick answer, but fail, themselves, to see the enormity of the problem.

Sometimes we're stubborn and selfish. It's sin that causes us not to experience this love in our lives. That's a fundamental answer. . .and it's important that we face it. My failure to love others with God's love is rooted in my sinful, selfish nature. Often I want to be loved before I am willing to give it.

Many people suffer from a family background that was not loving. When parents do not love their children or display love between themselves, the children suffer. When the children become adults, they have often been programmed to be unloving by their parents. Sometimes adults love in the wrong way because of past experiences that have not been wholesome and loving the way God intends us to love.

When discussing with one man about his lack of affection for his own children, he quickly answered with the example of his own parents. He had learned to avoid physical affection (demonstrating love) with his children from his own parents, who never showed him that kind of affection. He felt that fathers who did that were not strong, and were actually spoiling their children. I felt sorry for him. His children were suffering because of his beliefs.

Children can learn much about love when they see it in the lives of their parents. Much of today's home life is saturated with argument, bitterness, silence, withdrawal, and unfortunately for many, divorce. No wonder that many people have difficulty in understanding and manifesting love in their relationships with others.

Some are insecure in themselves due to past hurts and difficulties. It is hard for them to love because they are suspicious, or protective of themselves and their own family. They rarely reach out to other people. They are afraid to love. There is always a risk to take, a danger to face. What if the love is rejected or ignored? Can you remember how you felt when you tried to express a loving word or act to someone and they did not receive it well? Maybe they hurt you verbally, or just by their silence. If that happens to you often enough, you stop trying to love others. You withdraw, become insecure, and very private.

Many of us have problems loving because we have conditions. We love only if . . . Sometimes that is learned in our childhood. When a parent says, "You do this, and mother will love you," the child grows up believing that there are conditions to be met before one can experience love. Often you feel that you can never measure up. Many children believe that they are loved only when what they do meets with the approval of their parents. They do things to please their parents in order to receive a measure of love. That often carries over into adult life. Adults will dress a certain way, hoping for the approval of others. They will do constant acts of kindness and service in order to receive loving approval and response from others. When it doesn't come, the hurt gets deeper, and it becomes more difficult to love God's way.

Some find it difficult to love because of the way they have been used (or abused!) in the past. One teenage girl who had great insecurity in her relationships with others had learned to withdraw and isolate herself because of the way she was treated. She was physically mature at an early age, and became greatly enamoured with the affection of boys (That happens, you know!). Having had little physical affection from her parents, she responded quickly to what the boys were giving her. One thing led to another, and before long she was "going all the way" with several boys. After a few weeks of this kind of encounters, the boys dropped her. She was being used for sexual gratification, and it finally got to her. As she got older, she naturally became more suspicious and bitter, rarely showing any love for anyone. God's *LOVE* helped her to find acceptance and worth based on right principles.

There is a fine line between love and hate, but there is a line! I have witnessed an enormous amount of hate between married couples who supposedly love one another. They become indignant when you suggest that there is a lack of love in their relationship. They fight, argue, and shout at each other (some engage in physical abuse - hitting, kicking, and throwing things at each other - a few do things that result in tragedy, serious injury, and death!). When verbal abuse and attack continues in a marriage, is that a relationship based on love? Hardly! If love is present, it is certainly well-disguised! God's *LOVE* does not react in that way - ever!

Ephesians 4:31-32 says it clearly:

> "Let all bitterness and wrath and anger and clamor and slander be put away from you, along with all malice. And be kind to one another, tender-hearted, forgiving each other, just as God in Christ also has forgiven you."

It is quite difficult to love another person when we set some kind of standards that determine their worthiness to be loved. God loves us as we are, knowing fully our weaknesses and sins. When we are unlovely, He still loves us. His love is not dependent upon our performance or worthiness. We often have the "perfect person" in our minds whom we would enjoy loving. We see people in a certain light, and if they don't measure up, we don't express love to them.

I got excited one day at the office about "making love" to my wife. I felt very romantic and had in my mind what she looked like and how she would respond. I stopped at the florist and bought one rose, and put it in a lovely vase. I bought a very romantic card, and had great plans for the evening. When I got home, I could just imagine how my wife was going to respond. I even thought of how great it would be if she met me at the door in one of those sexy nightgowns (I buy a lot of them! I think I buy them for me, not her - that's my problem!). At the height of my anticipation, I opened the door, walked in, and said, "Honey, I'm home!" No response. She was lying down, not feeling well. Her hair was up in curlers, and she hadn't had an opportunity to get her bath yet - no makeup - and to top it off, wearing an old robe I really don't like! Terrific! Needless to say, my "romantic" ideas deteriorated rather rapidly! All of a sudden, I didn't feel "loving" anymore. I was upset, and I'm afraid it showed!

We all have experiences like that that reveal the depth and quality of our love. God's *LOVE* is always there - it's reliable, and you can count on it.

The place to start

If you want to know and experience God's *LOVE*, you're on the right track. Wanting it is where it all begins. Many of us don't sense our need of God's *LOVE*, so we ignore our problems and neglect our responsibility to love. Here are a few suggestions for those of you who really want to experience God's *LOVE* in your life, and you want to know where to start.

1. Admit that you are sinful and selfish, and thus, incapable of loving the way God wants.

I know that may sound strange to you, but you have to begin there. Sometimes our pride stands in the way. We think there's nothing wrong with us, and that with a little self-effort, we can love the way God wants us to love. Not a chance! His *LOVE* is different. It comes from a divine source, and is not produced by selfish effort and human motivation.

It's very liberating to admit your selfishness, pride, and sin. Confession of what you are is the beginning of true healing and restoration. Proverbs 28:13 says: "He who conceals his transgressions will not prosper, but he who confesses and forsakes them will find compassion."

2. Recognize that God's *LOVE* is available only to believers in Jesus Christ, and that it is produced by the Holy Spirit.

You can never know the deep satisfaction of loving God's way until you first of all, believe in Jesus Christ as your Lord and Saviour from sin. He died on the cross, paying for your sin (past, present, and future). Your sin was laid on Him, and the Bible teaches that forgiveness (one of the great qualities of God's *LOVE*) comes to you through belief in what Jesus Christ has already done. When He said, "It is finished," it meant that nothing could be added to what He did on that cross. You can't earn your way into God's favor. You can't pay for it, and you certainly don't deserve it! You must accept what Jesus Christ has already done at the cross over 1900 years ago.

When you do decide to believe on Jesus Christ, God places His Holy Spirit in you. It is the Spirit Who loves through us. Every believer has the Holy Spirit (I Corinthians 6:19; Romans 8:9), but that doesn't mean that the Holy Spirit has you (in the sense of controlling you - called the "filling of the Spirit" in Ephesians 5:18)! The capacity to love with God's *LOVE* is available to every believer. We have the potential. I John 4:19 says, "We love, because He first loved us." The problem lies in the fact that as believers we still have our old sin nature with which we were born. Now there is a struggle (a war at times!) that goes on inside the believer - a struggle between the Spirit and the flesh (Galatians 5:16-17). This brings us to a third point.

3. Realize that your old sin nature (selfish in every way) needs to be controlled.

Galatians 5:16 says, "But I say, walk by the Spirit, and you will not carry out the desire (lust) of the flesh." It does not say that you will no longer have the "desire of the flesh." If the Spirit is controlling you, you won't carry out what you desire in actual deeds.

But, how does one "walk by the Spirit?" That question is basic to living the Christian life. It is answered in many different ways by various Christian teachers. Things like more prayer, Bible study, witnessing, etc., are offered as possible answers. All of them are good and proper for Christians to do. But, how much is "more"? Every believer could use a little "more" of commitment in every area of life. To "walk" is to go step by step. It refers to being obedient to what the Spirit says. What the Spirit says is in the Word of God. He is the real Author of the Bible. If we are "walking by the Spirit" we are daily obeying what the Bible says. Let's state it in another way.

4. Respond to what the Bible says you should do, regardless of how you feel.

Many people do not experience God's *LOVE* because they depend upon their feelings. That's dangerous! My feelings change constantly. It is technically possible to love someone with God's *LOVE* even when you don't feel like it. Jesus said, "If you love Me, you will keep My command-ments (John 14:15)." Obedience is at the heart of God's *LOVE*. I show love to another person when I obey the Word of God's instruction as to how to respond to that person. When I do what is right, I am demonstrating love. When I respond to feelings of so-called "love," I often do the wrong thing, and wind up violating God's Word (all in the name of love!).

One young man shared with me his strong feelings of love for a certain young lady. Unfortunately, these feelings led him to become involved with her sexually (They were not married!). He reassured me that he really "loved" her or he would not "feel" as he did. I told him that his actions toward her could really reveal a lack of God's *LOVE*. Instead of caring for her the way he should, protecting her from many future problems which would result from their sexual involvement, he was controlled by his feelings at the moment. We often sacrifice the permanent on the altar of the immediate. That young man began to see that refraining from sexual involvement before marriage was indeed an expression of God's *LOVE*. His feelings did not change. When he was with her, he still felt sexual desire for her. But now, he was learning to express God's *LOVE* by obeying God's Word (which forbids sexual intercourse before marriage) in spite of the way he felt.

Does that mean that you will never have the "feelings" of love when you love with God's *LOVE*? Of course not. Feelings do come and they do exist. But, they should not control what we do or do not do. When we are obedient to God's Word, proper feelings will result.

All of this discussion points to why a study of I Corinthians 13 is so important. God's *LOVE* is being described in great detail in this chapter. If we want to express God's *LOVE* (the highest fulfillment) then we must learn to be obedient to what this chapter teaches.

Comments on the context

I Corinthians 13 is located in a book written to a group of believers who were not walking with the Lord. Chapter 3, verse 3, calls them "fleshly (carnal)." They were known for following their own selfish desires. It led them into a great many problems. In this church, the people were divided in their opinions and desires. They liked different speakers, and showed great dislike for others who felt otherwise. They were tolerating immorality in their church (incest), and had wrong ideas about divorce and marriage. They were not loving in their attitudes toward believers who felt differently about what kind of foods they should eat, or where they should be eaten. They were coveting special gifts of the Holy Spirit in order to be seen and to appear important. Some people with certain gifts were totally ignored and even despised because they did not have certain gifts that were treated as being the "best." This church had problems with the teaching about bodily resurrection and the need of systematic Christian giving. What a church! Most pastors I know would not care to pastor that kind of church!

The immediate context of I Corinthians 13 is a discussion about spiritual gifts. Chapters 12 and 14 go into great detail about the use (or misuse) of gifts. A list of gifts is given in chapter 12 (you'll find others listed in Romans 12, Ephesians 4, and I Peter 4), and an evaluation is made in chapter 14 of the gifts of tongues and prophecy. Gifts are given to the believers to use in ministering to other believers. It is the way that we are to "build up" one another in the body of Christ (Ephesians 4:12-16). Every believer has at least one spiritual gift (I Peter 4:10), and every believer is needed in the exercise of those gifts (I Corinthians 12:20-27). The problem at Corinth was a lack of love in the ministry of using spiritual gifts.

The key verse

The last verse of chapter 12 is the key verse that unlocks the context behind the "love chapter (13)." It says, "But earnestly desire the greater gifts. And I show you a still more excellent way." Many viewpoints have been expressed about this verse as it relates to chapter 13. For our understanding, and to prepare us for the study of this chapter, we need to establish a few points.

1. The verb translated "earnestly desire (be zealous)" can be either a command or a simple statement of fact. The grammatical form in Greek allows for either. The verse could be telling us to desire the greater gifts, or it could be simply stating the fact that the Corinthians were desiring the greater gifts. The difference could be quite important to the context and understanding of this discussion. Is Paul (the writer) condemning the Corinthians for desiring the greater gifts, or is he encouraging them to desire the greater gifts? Is he telling them that what they were doing was wrong and in violation of God's LOVE, or was he telling them to desire certain gifts (which they were not doing) and also to emphasize God's LOVE?

2. The Corinthian problem was that they were "carnal" and were misusing the gifts, not caring about the unity of the body or the purpose of the gifts. This seems obvious

from the discussion in chapter 12. The evaluation in chapter 14 could be emphasizing the need of a "greater gift" to be used in their church (which would obviously be "prophecy") rather than a "lesser gift" (which would refer to "tongues"). If that is true, then the words "earnestly desire the greater gifts" could be a command, pointing out that certain gifts (like prophecy) were more important than other gifts (like tongues).

3. The words "a more excellent *way*" emphasize that God's *LOVE* is a lifestyle, not simply a momentary act, or a moment's feeling. It is a way of doing things - a habit of life. It is easy to think of love being expressed at a given point in time (and it certainly is!), but the more difficult understanding is that God's *LOVE* is a way of life!

4. The words "more excellent" come from a Greek word (hyperbole) which we use in English for an "exaggeration," or overstating your point for emphasis. The way of God's *LOVE* needs to be exaggerated for emphasis! In one sense, you cannot overstate the case about God's *LOVE* - it is the greatest! Nothing in life can equal it!

5. God's *LOVE* is obviously greater than all the gifts. Chapter 13 will show us why.

6. The word "greater" (Greek - meidzon) is used of that which has excellence, worth, or importance. The "greater gifts" could refer to things listed in I Corinthians 12 or to prophecy as compared to tongues in chapter 14. If the "greater gifts" are the ones in chapter 12, then it might refer to the order or sequence that is mentioned in verses 28-30 (which immediately precede verse 31 - our key verse!). If this is the meaning of "greater gifts" then the first on the list would be "apostles" and the second "prophets," and the third "teachers." The other gifts would follow in order of importance.

Chapter 14, verse 1, seems to indicate that the believers are to "desire" spiritual gifts (or be zealous or enthusiastic about them), but to concentrate in a special way upon the gift of prophesying (or proclaiming God's message). Some Christians interpret the word "desire" as meaning that by your own personal desire you can acquire a certain spiritual gift. That is a mistake. Whatever gift you have is given by the sovereign distribution of the Holy Spirit (I Corinthians 12:11). The meaning of "desire" is not "to acquire," but to be "enthusiastic" or "zealous." In other words, Paul is teaching that spiritual gifts are important, but some have greater profit than others (prophecy over tongues, for example - chapter 14). That which we are to pursue and to follow with all our hearts is God's *LOVE* (I Corinthians 14:1).

Verse 31 of chapter 12, therefore, is urging the believers to be more enthusiastic for the greater gifts than the lesser gifts. The greater gifts are those that are used in proclaiming God's message to others, whether it be the "apostles, prophets, and teachers" or the gift of "prophecy."

7. The words of I Corinthians 12:31, ". . . I show you . . ." prove that God's *LOVE* can be seen and demonstrated. You can know this *LOVE* of God. It is evident. A life that loves like I Corinthians 13 will be evident to everyone!

The three paragraphs

I Corinthians 13 is composed of three paragraphs in Greek. The first includes verses 1-3; the second, verses 4-7; and the third, verses 8-13. What do these three paragraphs (three lines of thought) "show" us about God's *LOVE*?

Paragraph #1 - shows that God's LOVE is necessary for all Christian ministry!

Paragraph #2 - shows that God's LOVE is different from natural human behavior!

Paragraph #3 - shows that God's LOVE is greater than the gifts!

Paragraph #1 (verses 1-3) gives three reasons why God's *LOVE* is so necessary for all Christian ministry:

(1) Because without God's *LOVE*, your communication is ineffective - verse 1.

(2) Because without God's *LOVE*, your spiritual understanding is incomplete - verse 2.

(3) Because without God's *LOVE*, your sacrificial giving is insufficient - verse 3.

One phrase is repeated three times in the first paragraph - "but do not have love." This repeated phrase makes it clear that there are three lines of thought in the paragraph which the verse divisions clearly reveal. This phrase also shows the possibility of using these gifts without God's *LOVE!*

The word "if" in these verses suggests the thought that all of these examples are hypothetical. No one is really like these statements, but even if they were, without God's *LOVE*, the results are nothing!

The conclusions in paragraph 1 are all different.

Verse 1 - "I have become . . ." (This reveals what will happen to you without God's *LOVE*.)

Verse 2 - "I am nothing." (This shows that self-worth and self-esteem are based on God's *LOVE* in your life.)

Verse 3 - "It profits me nothing." (This reveals the results of giving without *LOVE*.)

Paragraph #2 (verses 4-7) is the heart of the description on God's *LOVE*. These verses are a gold mine of information of love. But, as with most of God's blessings, they must be applied. That's not so easy to do! Consider the following observations about paragraph #2:

1. The word *"LOVE"* (Greek has the definite article "the" in front of *"LOVE"*) is used just twice in the paragraph, both times with the first two statements. God's *LOVE* is beautifully summarized in the first two qualities: patience and kindness. Everything else that is said describes those two qualities in action.

2. After stating two positives, eight negative statements follow, showing us what God's *LOVE* is not. We often learn best what something is, by knowing what it is not.

3. Verse 7 makes four statements about God's *LOVE* as it relates to "all things." This verse tells us how God's *LOVE* reacts to all the changing circumstances and situations that we must inevitably face in life.

4. Only 41 words in Greek comprise this beautiful description of God's *LOVE* (61 words in English - NASB).

5. All of the verbs (15 of them in Greek) are in the

present tense, a tense which indicates a continual habit of life. God's *LOVE* is truly a "way" of life (I Corinthians 12:31)!

Paragraph #2 gives us three ways in which God's *LOVE* is different from natural human behavior: First - God's *LOVE* is different in its response toward people - verse 4a. Secondly - God's *LOVE* is different in its refusal to act with selfish attitudes - verses 4b-6. Thirdly - God's *LOVE* is different in its reaction to circumstances - verse 7.

Paragraph #3 (verses 8-13) reveals two ways in which God's *LOVE* is greater than all the gifts: First - God's *LOVE* is greater in future endurance. The key phrase here is "love never fails" (verse 8). The gifts will not last forever, and that argument is unfolded in verses 8-12. Secondly - God's *LOVE* is greater in present experience. Verse 13 tells us that "faith, hope, and love" are now abiding (present) in our lives, but that God's *LOVE* is the greatest of them all!

All of these comments about the context of I Corinthians 13 are intended to give us understanding about the teaching on God's *LOVE*. But, if you are not experiencing God's *LOVE*, and you want to, then go back to the section titled, "THE PLACE TO START," and read again what was said, and apply those four principles in your life. In some ways, that particular section is the most important one in the whole book!

The love chapter - I Corinthians 13

If I speak with the tongues of men and of angels,
> but do not have love,
>> I have become a noisy gong or a clanging cymbal.

And if I have the gift of prophecy, and know all mysteries and all knowledge; and if I have all faith, so as to remove mountains,
> but do not have love,
>> I am nothing.

And if I give all my possessions to feed the poor, and if I deliver my body to be burned,
> but do not have love,
>> it profits me nothing.

Love is patient, love is kind,
> and is not jealous;
> love does not brag
> and is not arrogant,
> does not act unbecomingly;
> it does not seek its own,
> is not provoked,
> does not take into account a wrong suffered,
> does not rejoice in unrighteousness, but rejoices with
> the truth;
>> bears all things,
>> believes all things,
>> hopes all things,
>> endures all things.

Love never fails;
> but if there are gifts of prophecy,
>> they will be done away;
> if there are tongues,
>> they will cease;
> if there is knowledge,
>> it will be done away.

For we know in part, and we prophesy in part;
> but when the perfect comes,
> the partial will be done away.

When I was a child, I used to
>> speak as a child,
>> think as a child,
>> reason as a child;

When I became a man,
> I did away with childish things.

For now we see in a mirror dimly,
> but then face to face;
>> now I know in part,
> but then I shall know fully just as I also have been fully
> known.

But now abide faith, hope, love, these three;
> **But the greatest of these is love.**

Pursue
Love
IT'S YOUR GREATEST NEED
FIRST CORINTHIANS 13

PART ONE

LOVE IS NECESSARY FOR ALL CHRISTIAN MINISTRY . . .

Because without love . . .

1. Your communication is ineffective.
   I Corinthians 13:1

2. Your spiritual understanding is incomplete.
   I Corinthians 13:2

3. Your sacrificial giving is insufficient.
   I Corinthians 13:3

1 | Why your communication is ineffective

"If I speak with the tongues of men and of angels, but do not have love, I have become a noisy gong or a clanging cymbal."

- I Corinthians 13:1

"Tongues" normally refers to languages. The word in Greek (*glossais*) appears 50 times in the New Testament in its various forms. Even if you could speak all the languages of the world known to mankind, without *LOVE*, we are unimpressed. Linguistic ability is a wonderful talent, and most valuable. World travel has brought people of different languages more closely together. But, *LOVE* is the best language of all. It communicates when eloquence doesn't.

The "tongues of angels" would be a more difficult skill than the "tongues of men." What language do they speak? When angels spoke to people in Bible times, it appears they spoke in the language of the people they were talking to - Hebrew, Aramaic, Greek - it didn't seem to hold them back. Some people say that the "tongues of angels" refer to heavenly language, and that the gift of tongues was that ability.

Paul was caught up to the third heaven (Paradise - II Corinthians 12:2,4) where God dwells. According to II Corinthians 12:4, he heard ". . . inexpressible words, which a man is not permitted to speak." The language of heaven was too difficult to repeat, and was not even allowed among humans! But, even if you could speak the "tongues of angels," without *LOVE*, the results are tragic - you have become a "noisy gong or a clanging cymbal." Often, we put the emphasis on the wrong thing. Beautiful language, wonderful eloquence, effective speaking - they are all gifts from God, but without *LOVE*, they are ineffective.

LOVE is the great need in communication! Several years ago I was listening to a great speaker who was trying to impress his audience with his speaking ability. There was little love in what he said. It was tragic. I thought then as I think now - without *LOVE*, real communication does not take place.

The words "I have become" indicate that the person's life was not always like this. He is responsible for this change. It's a simple reminder of how easy it is to slip from a Spirit-filled life of *LOVE* to one that is mere noise. These words also indicate that it is now a habit. How easy it is to develop a habit of speaking without love. You say all the right words, but something is missing - God's *LOVE!*

One day I was trying desperately to get my point across to one of my children. I raised my voice, and spoke with great authority. My child responded, "Do you love me, Daddy?" That hurt! Of course I love my child, but at that moment, it was not coming through due to the manner in which I was speaking. My overall commitment is based on love for my child, but on that occasion, the manner of my speaking was indicating the opposite.

Ephesians 4:15 urges us to "speak the truth in love." That's a difficult assignment at times! Suppose a lady would ask you what you thought of her new dress, and suppose it was really ugly on her. How would you tell her? Would you lie and say, "It's beautiful on you!" That's not Biblical love! Would you say, "You look terrible in that . . . whatever made you buy it?" That doesn't sound too loving! To speak the truth in love requires some thought. Learn to compliment the person as well as communicate the truth. Perhaps something like this would help: "For someone as attractive as you are, it doesn't do much for you!" Or, "I think that dress detracts from the good qualities you have!" (If you don't like those responses - come up with your own!) In other words, show appreciation sincerely for the real person as well as communicating the truth as you see it.

"A noisy gong" refers to echoing brass. It indicates a constant and powerful repetition. One night at a church concert I was sitting on the platform in front of the percussion section of the orchestra. Right in back of me was the person with the cymbals. When those cymbals came together, the sound wasn't too pleasant to my ears! I kept hearing that echoing sound, and it was not enjoyable. That's what it's like when you are speaking to someone without God's *LOVE*. The sound hurts more than it helps.

"A clanging cymbal" is based upon Greek words used for crying and weeping loudly over the dead. Somehow that's the way it sounds when you try to communicate without *LOVE*. It causes grief and sadness, rather than joy.

Husbands are told in Colossians 3:19 to "love your wives, and do not be embittered against them." Literally it means "stop being sharp toward your wives." The root word means "to cut" or "to prick." Speaking without *LOVE* is like that. Many marriages are suffering because of bad communication on the part of the husband as well as the wife. There is a danger of not communicating with one another. There is another danger of communicating in the wrong way - without *LOVE*!

When you love someone, you can say most anything to them. Even when they don't agree with what you said, they still love you for trying! I was going through that over the phone one day. The person I was talking with had unbelievable problems in her life. I cared about her very much, but I just didn't have the answers she was seeking. She knew it, and I knew it (and I was her pastor!). A few days later she told me how much our conversation meant to her. She said, "You didn't have any answers, but I knew that you cared about me, and that was what I needed at that time." Well, not every situation works out like that. Often, I am unloving and uncaring, and I'm afraid it shows!

Ephesians 4:25-5:2 is a powerful section on the way we

talk and the need for love in our speech. We are exhorted to speak words that will build people up not tear them down. We are told to remove all bitterness, wrath, anger, clamor, slander, and all malice from our speech. We are to be kind and forgiving. We are to walk in love as Christ has loved us; for without God's *LOVE*, our communication will be ineffective!

2 | What's lacking in your spiritual understanding?

"And if I have the gift of prophecy, and know all mysteries and all knowledge; and if I have all faith, so as to remove mountains, but do not have love, I am nothing."

- I Corinthians 13:2

Spiritual understanding is a wonderful thing! Too many people are immature and even unnecessarily ignorant in their comprehension of spiritual and Biblical truth. But, spiritual understanding is not the highest good. It can even be deficient, though it is comprehensive. The missing ingredient may be *LOVE*. Without God's *LOVE*, your spiritual understanding is incomplete. That's the point behind verse two.

The words *"the gift of"* are in italics, which means that they are not found in the Greek text. It's an interpretation of what is meant.

"Prophecy" refers to the content of God's revelation to man. The whole Bible is "prophecy." Peter spoke about this in II Peter 1:19-21:

"And so we have the prophetic word made more sure, to which you do well to pay attention as to a lamp shining in a dark place, until the day dawns and the morning star arises in your hearts. But know this first of all, that no prophecy of Scripture is a matter of one's own interpretation, for no prophecy was ever made by an act of human will, but men moved by the Holy Spirit spoke from God."

John said in Revelation 22:18-19 that no man could take

away or add to the words of the "prophecy" of this book. The Bible is "prophecy."

The word "prophecy" means "predicting the future" to most of us today. That was not its primary meaning. The Greek form of the word means "to speak before." Not only speaking before an event occurred, but also, it means speaking before a crowd of people. It refers to public speaking or proclamation. A "prophet" was a mouthpiece, speaking forth what he was told.

The gift of prophesying was obviously very important in the early church (it is today also!). I Corinthians 14:3 says, "But one who prophesies speaks to men for edification and exhortation and consolation." In verse 4 it tells us that one who prophesies "edifies the church."

However, even if you have the gift of proclaiming God's truth, but you don't have God's *LOVE*, the Bible says you are nothing - a big zero! Your worth is at an all-time low when you don't have God's *LOVE*!

The phrase "know all mysteries" is certainly comprehensive - "all" indicates that this person has really arrived in terms of spiritual understanding. The "mysteries" refer to everything God has kept as a secret in the past, waiting for the proper time to reveal them.

"All knowledge," of course, refers to everything there is to know. Specifically, it probably refers to all that God wants us to know. Even if this were possible (and it is not!), without God's *LOVE* in your life, you are nothing.

No verse so disturbs the Christian scholar and student like this one. There are so few believers who really study as they should. When one comes along who is a real student of the Word, it is refreshing to see. People will flock to hear someone like that who really knows what he is talking about. But without *LOVE*, he is nothing. That's hard to accept, but it is true. I Corinthians 8:1 says, ". . . Knowledge makes arrogant, but *LOVE* edifies." It's important to know, but without *LOVE* there is no ministry of building up. Believers are built up (encouraged) in the sphere of God's *LOVE* (Ephesians 4:16).

God puts no premium on ignorance, but He doesn't honor knowledge without love either. The formula should be "Knowledge + Love." They go together. Both are needed. The most important, and truly the greatest, however, is LOVE!

"Removing mountains" is no small task! It takes great faith. What kind of faith is under discussion here? It is a little difficult to be dogmatic, but here are a few suggestions.

First, the concept of faith removing mountains is used in Matthew 17:20. The problem in that passage was the inability of the disciples to cast out a demon from an epileptic boy. Jesus said that they lacked faith.

There is a spiritual gift mentioned in I Corinthians 12:9 called "faith." Could this be the ability to cast out demons? In Mark 16:17-18 Jesus mentioned some miraculous things that the apostles would be able to do. One of them was to "cast out demons." Since he mentioned that they would "speak with new tongues" (and that is obviously one of the spiritual gifts of I Corinthians 12), could it not be that the ability to cast out demons was also one of the spiritual gifts, namely, faith?

Secondly, another usage of faith removing mountains is found in Matthew 21:21. The background here was the ability of Jesus to cause a fig tree to wither by simply speaking a word of condemnation to it for not having figs, but only leaves.

Thirdly, without faith, we cannot please God (Hebrews 11:6), so there is a sense in which all believers must have faith, even though not all believers have the spiritual gift of faith. Believers must have faith when they become believers as well as in living the Christian life. We walk by faith according to Colossians 2:6.

Fourthly, some believers have more faith than others, regardless of whether or not they have the spiritual gift of faith. Our faith grows as we rely upon God and His Word. Those who are spiritually mature will have more faith at times than those who are new converts.

Lastly, in Hebrews 11:32-40 it appears that faith is the

ability to trust God in difficult circumstances. The believers of the past were able to endure much suffering and persecution because of faith.

Faith that removes mountains seems to be of a more miraculous nature than other kinds of faith. Whether it is the ability to cast out demons (as it was in Matthew 17:20) or cause a fig tree to wither (Matthew 21:21), we do not know. It might apply to many kinds of situations. The point of I Corinthians 13:2 is that even if you had "all" faith that any person could possibly display in his life, but you did not have God's *LOVE*, you are nothing.

Prophecy, mysteries, knowledge, faith - all wonderful gifts! But, without God's *LOVE*, you are nothing though you have them all! This reveals what is really wrong with many people who claim to have great spiritual understanding but who rarely affect people in a positive, encouraging way. People could care less about what they know. They see little evidence of love in their lives and so they don't respond.

Maybe that's what is wrong in your life! It's easy to be satisfied with your spiritual knowledge. It's rather simple to be confident that you are on the right track when you have so much knowledge. But, being right all the time on every issue does not mean that you have a ministry in the lives of others. Without *LOVE*, there are few results.

I had a friend like that. He was usually right on every thing. He loved to study and to learn new truths. He talked about knowing the truth and making sure of what the Bible said in every single passage. That is, of course, an important thing. What is true is not what I think, but what God's Word says. Somehow, however, people did not respond to him. He felt very lonely. When he talked, people got bored, and turned him off. He wanted to tell others what he knew, and he knew plenty. But his problem was that he did not love. People could feel that, and it was hard for them to listen to him because of it. I have seen that problem in many people, including myself. I love to study and to learn. I always have. One thing I still need to learn is how to love people with God's *LOVE*.

Don't misread what has been said! Knowledge and spiritual understanding are important. Don't excuse yourself by saying that since knowledge without love is not effective, you won't learn anymore! We must continue to learn and grow mentally. But in the process, we must learn more of God's *LOVE*. Our own self-worth and image is related to it. The phrase "I am nothing" indicates the real truth. God's *LOVE* establishes your worth. He loves us when we are so unlovely. Our love for others will also build their self-image and worth. Nothing is so encouraging or up-building than to experience the *LOVE* of God through another believer's life and ministry.

What's wrong with sacrificial giving? | 3

"And if I give all my possessions to feed the poor, and if I deliver my body to be burned, but do not have love, it profits me nothing."

- I Corinthians 13:3

This is philanthropy at its best. Talk about "social consciousness!" Here is evidence of human concern for the poor of this world. But, without God's *LOVE*, there's no profit. Without God's *LOVE*, your sacrificial giving is insufficient, and does not produce proper results. The words *"the poor"* are in italics meaning that they are not in the Greek text. The verb "to feed" literally means "to feed by little bits." It is used of feeding children and young animals. In modern Greek, the word refers to "bread" and the verb means "to shop."

Spiros Zodhiates in his wonderful book, *To Love is to Live*, makes this statement:

"It does not follow that the more we give away the more we shall love God, but rather that the more we love God, the more we shall be willing to give away. What we do is always the result of what we are. To give because we believe that in this way we shall enjoy more of God's blessing and God Himself is loveless charity."

II Corinthians 8:5 states that the Macedonian believers (poor financially, but rich spiritually) demonstrated the real priority in all Christian giving: ". . . they first gave themselves to the Lord . . ."

To give "all my possessions" suggests a tremendous commitment. Most of us give only a portion of our income. Frequently, what we give is so small, we don't sense any sacrifice at all. To give everything away shows a great deal of dedication. But, without God's *LOVE*, there is no profit in it. That's difficult to believe - but that's what God's word says. You can give without *LOVE*, but you cannot *LOVE* without giving! Don't stop giving, but start loving!

I thought about the importance of love one day when a little child in our church sent me a note which said, "I love you, Pastor, and here's a quarter - take your family out to lunch!" That quarter was special to me. It wasn't enough to pay for lunch, but I didn't care - the thought behind it was worth much more.

The poor widow of Luke 21:1-4 gave two small copper coins (*lepta*), and it didn't seem like much in comparison to all the rich putting their gifts into the temple treasury. But Jesus said, "Truly I say to you, this poor widow put in more than all of them; for they all out of their surplus put into the offering; but she out of her poverty put in all she had to live on."

The phrase "if I deliver my body to be burned" is based on late readings of the manuscript evidence available on this passage. Earlier readings contain the words "that I might boast." The difference between "burned" and "boast" is only one letter in Greek. Copiers could have easily made this mistake. The oldest manuscripts (not necessarily the best by any means!) contain the reading "to boast."

The statement could be referring to the giving of oneself as a slave would do by necessity. In this case, you would give yourself out of choice, not compulsion. Paul spoke of giving (or presenting) your body to God for His service (Romans 12:1).

Some see this statement as referring to the act of martyrdom. They rely on the manuscript evidence that translates "if I deliver my body to be burned." However, it seems to this writer, that the words "that I might boast" fit better in the context.

Many of us have the ability to make great dedications and sacrifices. We can give ourselves to great causes. But often the motive is selfish - we are "boasting." We take great pride in our commitment. That's not the way God's *LOVE* works.

Matthew 6:1-4 warns us about doing things to be seen by others. Our commitment to give is to be "in secret." Our heavenly Father Who sees in secret will reward us in His time and in His way.

In examining this verse about sacrificial giving, it seems that two things are revealed: First, your purpose in giving reveals whether there is love or not - "that I might boast." If your purpose is to brag on yourself as to how great a person you are because of what you have done, then you lack God's *LOVE* in your life. Secondly, the profit you receive in giving is not found in what was given (as to amount or cost), but in the motive behind it - *LOVE*! We pay too much attention to the size of the gift rather than the motive behind the gift. The great profit is not found in the size, but in the "why."

In these days of inflation, the size of the gift becomes increasingly important to people. But God is not broke. Costs may escalate, but God's method of evaluation remains the same. The Lord is more interested in your motives than in the amounts. Many of us give because we want to receive. That reveals the lack of *LOVE* in our hearts.

What's wrong with sacrificial giving? Nothing, if there is *LOVE* behind it; everything, if there is no *LOVE*. John 3:16 reminds us that "God so loved the world, that He gave His only begotten Son . . ." John 15:13 says, "Greater love has no one than this, that one lay down his life for his friends." I John 3:16-18 adds:

> "We know love by this, that He laid down His life for us; and we ought to lay down our lives for the brethren. But whoever has the world's goods, and beholds his brother in need and closes his heart against him, how does the love of God abide in him? Little children, let us not love with word or with

tongue, but in deed and truth.''

God's *LOVE* will give, not just mouth the words. God's *LOVE* will make great sacrifices for the benefit of the object loved. But, it is possible to give and make great sacrifices without having any love in your heart. You can do it for yourself, either to strengthen your personal viewpoint of yourself, or to impress others with how wonderful a person you must be because of what you have given. There is no substitution for God's *LOVE* - it is our greatest need!

Pursue
love
IT'S YOUR GREATEST NEED
FIRST CORINTHIANS 13

PART TWO

LOVE IS DIFFERENT FROM NATURAL HUMAN BEHAVIOR

1. It is different in its response toward people.
   I Corinthians 13:4a

2. It is different in its refusal to act with selfish attitudes.
   I Corinthians 13:4b-6

3. It is different in its reaction to circumstances.
   I Corinthians 13:7

4 | How love responds to people

"Love is patient, love is kind"
- I Corinthians 13:4a

The second paragraph of this chapter (verses 4-7) reveals how love is different from natural human reaction and behavior patterns. When people try to define love, they usually define actions of which they are capable if they would only try. God's LOVE, which comes from Him and is produced by Him, is different from normal conduct. It responds to people in ways that are unexpected.

Two simple words describe how love is different in its response to people: patient and kind. These two positive statements show us what God's LOVE is, while the eight negative statements that follow show us what His LOVE is not. The 41 words in this paragraph are greater than all the essays, poems, and books written about love.

The definite article in Greek appears before the word "love" in each statement - *"the love,"* the particular one that comes from God. The only time the word "love" appears in this paragraph is with these two opening statements. It proves that they summarize the meaning of God's LOVE. When you have these two operating in your life as habits, then you are loving the way God intends you to love. Since they are the main qualities of God's LOVE, we will take some time to study their meanings.

Love is patient

If there was one quality which people seem to have a great deal of trouble with, it would be patience. The Greek word means "taking a long time to boil." It is translated "longsuffering." It is always used with respect to persons, not things or situations. There is a Greek word meaning "patience" that refers to things and circumstances that we must endure. It is found in verse 7, and we shall study its meaning and usage at that point. Here we are talking about being patient toward people. God is never said to be patient toward things. He doesn't need that kind of patience for He is controlling all things. The Bible does say that God is patient toward people (II Peter 3:9).

Patience toward people (longsuffering) is a fruit of the Spirit (Galatians 5:22). It is not natural to exhibit this patience; it requires divine help. It is normal to be quite impatient with the way people act and respond. I found myself quite upset one day with the way a certain person was doing a job I had asked him to do. I was very impatient with him because the speed at which he was doing this task was not the speed I was demanding. I felt sick inside when I realized my impatience was getting the best of me. When I sought God's help and confessed my sin, I noticed an immediate change in my attitude. The speed of that person no longer mattered. I was now happy that he was involved in helping me. After all, that's what really counts!

Needing God's help and admitting that you cannot handle things, is a first step to having patience. I Thessalonians 5:14 says that we are to ". . . be patient with all men." But, not everyone meets our standards or demands for experiencing our patience! It seems to me at times that people will do things that try our patience (Have you noticed?)!

God had patience while Noah was building the ark (I Peter 3:20). That generation deserved the judgment of God, but God was patient, giving them much opportunity to repent. After 120 years of preaching by Noah, God brought His judgment of a universal flood upon the earth. Genesis 6:3 reminds us, ". . . My spirit shall not strive with man forever, . . . '' God is patient with us. He takes a long time to boil (for which many of us are indeed thankful!). The root reason behind God's patience toward undeserving, rebellious people, is His great *LOVE*! Yes, *LOVE* is patient.

Examples of patience:

1. *God Himself* - He's the best example, obviously! His patience is revealed toward unbelievers as well as believers. He endures the wickedness and rebellion of unbelievers (Romans 9:22; I Peter 3:20), and He endures the unfaithfulness and sin of believers. The words ''slow to anger'' in many Old Testament passages are translated into the Greek word of I Corinthians 13:4, ''patient.'' His patience is often used in connection with His forgiveness. In Exodus 34:6-7, we read:

> "Then the Lord passed by in front of him and proclaimed, 'The Lord, the Lord God, compassionate and gracious, **slow to anger**, and abounding in lovingkindness and truth; who keeps lovingkindness for thousands, who **forgives** iniquity, transgression and sin; yet He will by no means leave the guilty unpunished, visiting the iniquity of fathers on the children and on the grandchildren to the third and fourth generations.'''

In Numbers 14:18-19, Moses prays this remarkable prayer:

> "The Lord is **slow to anger** and abundant in lovingkindness, **forgiving** iniquity and transgression; but He will by no means clear the guilty; visiting the iniquity of the fathers on the children to the third and the fourth generations. Pardon, I pray, the iniquity of this people according to the greatness of Thy lovingkindness, just as Thou also hast **forgiven** this people, from Egypt even until now."

There is a beautiful testimony to God's patience revealed in the words of Paul in I Timothy 1:15-16. It shows that patience is rooted in forgiveness and mercy toward sinful men.

> "It is a trustworthy statement, deserving full acceptance, that Christ Jesus came into the world to save sinners, among whom I am foremost of all. And yet for this reason I found mercy, in order that in me as the foremost, Jesus Christ might demonstrate His perfect

> **patience**, as an example for those who would believe
> in Him for eternal life.''

Our patience is usually tested when we run into unresponsive people. I remember well my lack of patience in dealing with a man who continued to fall back into habits of sin. Over and over again he would seem to repent, get right with God, and then sin again. It was one discouraging circle of events. I thought I loved him, and wanted to help, but I found myself becoming more and more impatient with his sinful ways and weaknesses. I know he had a problem, but so did I. I see my problem in better focus when I think of the patience of our Lord - no matter how many times we have fallen, He is there to forgive and to pick up the broken pieces. How I praise Him for His loving patience with me!

2. *A slave* - Matthew 18:21-35. Here is a lesson on forgiveness. Peter wanted to know how often we should forgive our brother who sins against us. He suggested seven times. The Lord replied with seventy times seven - or, to put it another way, with no limitation. Jesus then told a story about a king who wanted to settle accounts with his slaves. One owed him 10,000 talents, and did not have the means to repay. The king ordered him to be sold along with his wife and children and all that he had. Then, according to Matthew 18:26, the slave fell down before the king and said, "Have *patience* with me, and I will repay you everything." The king then felt compassion and forgave him. That slave then went to one of his fellow-slaves who owed him only 100 denarii. His fellow-slave fell down before him and begged him saying, "Have *patience* with me, and I will repay you." But he was not compassionate like his king, but threw him in prison until he would pay him back what was owed. When the king heard of it, he was angry and handed the first slave over to the torturers until he would repay his debt. Jesus commented on this whole incident by saying in Matthew 18:35, "So shall My heavenly Father also do to you, if each of you does not forgive his brother from your heart."

The meaning of "Love is patient" is definitely connected with the idea of forgiveness. We are not patient with people unless we are willing to forgive them for what they have done against us.

Consider these Old Testament passages dealing with patience or longsuffering. In each case, the words "slow to anger" are based on our word for "patience." The Greek Old Testament uses the word in I Corinthians 13:4 to translate the Hebrew word "slow to anger."

> Proverbs 14:29
> "He who is slow to anger has great understanding, but he who is quick-tempered exalts folly."
>
> Proverbs 15:18
> "A hot-tempered man stirs up strife, but the slow to anger pacifies contention."
>
> Proverbs 16:32
> "He who is slow to anger is better than the mighty, and he who rules his spirit, than he who captures a city."
>
> Proverbs 19:11
> "A man's discretion makes him slow to anger, and it is his glory to overlook a transgression."

In Acts 26:3 Paul was standing before King Agrippa and said, "because you are an expert in all customs and questions among the Jews; therefore I beg you to listen to me *patiently*." Paul simply wanted him to listen to his defense. Listening to others is often a manifestation of patience. God's *LOVE* is willing to listen even when it is not convenient or particularly enjoyable.

Ask yourself, "Am I patient with people?" If you are, then according to Biblical teaching, the following seven things will be true of your love: (1) you are slow to anger; (2) you are merciful (holding back wrath); (3) you are forgiving; (4) you are willing to listen; (5) you are able to endure the sins of others; (6) you are resting in God's plan and knowledge; (7) you don't give up on people.

Ephesians 4:1-3 tells us how believers should respond to each other. Verse two says, "with all humility and gentleness, with *patience*, showing forbearance to one another *in love.*" "Showing forbearance" means to "put up with one another." Everyone is different, and feels differently about things from the way you do. If you have God's *LOVE*, you will learn to put up with other people and their ways and viewpoints. You will exercise humility and gentleness in your dealings with them, always willing to forgive. It's not easy, but loving with God's *LOVE* never has been! But, it's the only way!

Love is kind

The Greek language uses the present tense and should be translated, "the love is continually kind." According to Galatians 5:22, it is a part of the "fruit of the Spirit." It is produced by the Spirit in the life of the believer. It does not come naturally to you to be kind.

The word comes from a root verb meaning "to take into use." It comes to mean that which is useful, serviceable, adapted to its purpose, and thus excellent or valuable. When referring to foods, it means that which is healthy or tasty. I like to think that God's *LOVE* is good for you (healthy), and is delicious to the taste!

There are frequent usages of this word in reference to oil and wine. It means "good" or "useful" in terms of cooking. A jar to hold wine is called "fit to use" and our word for "kind" is the adjective describing the jar. Wine that is mellowed by age is called "better" or "good enough" (Luke 5:39) and our word for "kind" is used in that context.

Examples of kindness

1. *God Himself* - no one is "kind" as God is. His kindness leads us to repentance (Romans 2:4). A good reminder to all of us - if we want to see people repent (change) of sin, a little loving kindness would help! God's kindness is based on His character, not our worthiness. An interesting usage of His kindness in this regard is found in Romans 11:19-22. It is God's kindness that makes the salva-

tion of Gentiles possible.

In Titus 3:3-7, it is God's kindness that saves us not on the basis of deeds we have done, but according to His mercy. The Greek translation of Nahum 1:7 says, "The Lord is *kind*, a stronghold in the day of trouble, . . . " Most English translations read, "The Lord is good, . . ."

2. *A king of Babylon* - a fascinating look into the meaning of kindness is found in Jeremiah 52:31-34. Evil-merodach, king of Babylon, showed kindness to Jehoiachin, king of Judah, by bringing him out of prison and exalting him. Verse 32 says, "Then he spoke kindly to him and set his throne above the thrones of the kings who were with him in Babylon." Verse 33 says that Jehoiachin had his meals with the king all the days of his life, and that a regular allowance was given to him until the day of his death (v. 34)! That's what I call kindness!

When you are kind, you have compassion on the needs of others, and you do something about it! What you do should be useful to them; only then is God's *LOVE* operating . . . only then are you really kind. Have you ever received a gift from someone that was really intended for them, not you? It was in no way useful to you, but rather for someone else. Was love shown to you? God's *LOVE* would be concerned about doing that which is useful for the object of that love, because it is kind.

3. *The yoke of Christ* - Matthew 11:28-30. Beautiful words of rest and peace are found in this passage. Christ invites us to "come" to Him for rest. Our responsibility is to "take" His yoke and begin learning from Him. Why? Because His yoke is "easy" and His burden is "light." The word translated "easy" is our word for "kind." It is the opposite of harsh, bitter, or burdensome. When you become a burden to others, you are not kind, and thus, not demonstrating the love of God. The ancient wooden yoke was strapped tightly to the experienced ox. The straps were loosely tied to the inexperienced ox who was to walk beside the experienced ox and learn how to plow - without bearing the load! Christ (the experienced ox) is bearing the load; we

(inexperienced oxen) are to walk beside Him and learn from Him - His yoke is "easy" (kind) and never a burden. Praise the Lord!

Ask yourself, "Am I a burden to people? Or, do I seek to lift their burdens?" When you talk to other believers, do you immediately unload all your problems on them? Do you spend most of the time talking about yourself, or do you rather seek to hear their burdens and share in their needs? God's *LOVE* is kind, and therefore, not burdensome.

4. *Believers attitude toward non-believers* - Luke 6:27-38 challenges believers to love their enemies and to do good to them that hate you. Verse 35 points out that our example is God Himself Who is *"kind* to ungrateful and evil men" The real test of your kindness comes when people do not respond to you. Where is God's *LOVE* when people treat you wrong? How do you react when non-believers show their hostility toward what you believe and how you live? Is it righteous indignation they see? Or, is it loving kindness?

5. *Believers' attitude toward each other* - Ephesians 4:32 says, "And be *kind* to one another, tender-hearted, forgiving each other, just as God in Christ also has forgiven you." Kindness is rooted in forgiveness, just as patience is. If you cannot forgive, you are not kind, and therefore, not loving with God's *LOVE*.

The most unkind act I can display toward a fellow believer is to refuse to forgive him or her for what was done to me. Knowing God's kindness to me through Jesus Christ, what else can I do but forgive?

If you are kind in your response toward people, then the following five things will characterize you: (1) you are forgiving; (2) you do what is useful and beneficial to others; (3) you respond with good even though others are undeserving and unresponsive; (4) you do not put burdens on people, but rather seek to relieve them; (5) you do not remember the sins of people, nor hold it against them.

Consider these passages from the Psalms on kindness.

Psalm 25:7-8
"Do not remember the sins of my youth or my transgressions; According to Thy lovingkindness remember
Thou me, For Thy goodness' sake, O Lord. Good
(**kind**) and upright is the Lord; Therefore He instructs
sinners in the way."

Psalm 31:19
"How great is Thy goodness (**kindness**), Which Thou
hast stored up for those who fear Thee, Which Thou
hast wrought for those who take refuge in Thee,
before the sons of men!"

Psalm 86:5
"For Thou, Lord, art good (**kind**), and ready to forgive,
and abundant in lovingkindness to all who call upon
Thee."

Psalm 100:5
"For the Lord is good (**kind**); His lovingkindness is
everlasting, and His faithfulness to all generations."

Psalm 106:1 and 107:1
"Oh give thanks to the Lord, for He is good (**kind**); for
His lovingkindness is everlasting."

Psalm 119:68
"Thou art good (**kind**) and doest good; Teach me Thy
statutes."

Psalm 145:7-9
"They shall eagerly utter the memory of Thine abun-
dant goodness (**kindness**), and shall shout joyfully of
Thy righteousness. The Lord is gracious and merciful;
Slow to anger (**patience**) and great in lovingkindness.
The Lord is good (**kind**) to all, and His mercies are
over all His works."

Patience and kindness are a summary of what God's
LOVE really is. Those two attributes of love tell us how to
respond to people. They are produced in the life of one who
is controlled (filled) by the Holy Spirit. They are very
different from natural human behavior. Our first response
to people is not patience or kindness - normally we are very
impatient and very unkind!

I get some nasty letters in the mail. It comes with the

job, I guess. Having a daily radio broadcast on several stations exposes one to many people. Some do not like what I say (nothing new!), and take the liberty to write me and unleash their fury against me. It's hard not to retaliate. People say things that I know are not true, but to them, they are true. When I face the task of writing a letter back I must keep asking myself the question - is this loving, or is it vindictive? Am I kind and patient in how I respond? Over the years I have not seen much good come from a sharp answer or a revengeful spirit. When we respond with *LOVE*, there is no answer. It often becomes the ''heat'' that God uses to melt a very cold heart. I would rather be known for being loving than for one who always wanted his own way (my natural inclination!).

5 | What love refuses to do

". . . is not jealous; love does not brag and is not arrogant, does not act unbecomingly; it does not seek its own, is not provoked, does not take into account a wrong suffered, does not rejoice in unrighteousness, but rejoices with the truth."

- I Corinthians 13:4b-6

Love is different from natural human behavior in its response toward people (patience and kindness), and in its refusal to act with selfish attitudes (eight negative statements - all telling us what love is not!).

All of these eight negative statements are in the present tense in Greek, meaning a habit or pattern of life. God's *LOVE* does not act this way as a habit of life. It doesn't mean that there won't be temporary setbacks or momentary failures to love. What it does mean is that your way of doing things, your habits, your consistent lifestyle is now governed by God's *LOVE* and not these eight negative statements.

It was a racquetball game, and I was mad. I was playing with a non-believer, but I was still upset! He was putting me down, and trying to rattle me (he was doing a good job!). Without thinking, and certainly without loving, I let off some steam. I proceeded to do what we commonly call "clean him off the court." I felt justified in doing it. After the game, I felt a deep hurt inside. I knew I had no love, and I probably hurt my chances of sharing Christ with him.

After some minutes had passed by, I went to him and asked him for his forgiveness. He was shocked and said it wasn't necessary, but I knew better. God's *LOVE* doesn't do what most people think is normal!

Love is not jealous

It does not say that it is okay to be jealous at times; it says that God's *LOVE* is not jealous - period! The Greek word means "to seethe" or "to boil." It is an emotional word, and can be used in a good or an evil sense. In a good sense it refers to "zeal" or "enthusiasm." In a bad sense, it carries the idea of bitterness and resentment, and much comparison to others.

Joseph's brothers were jealous of him. They hated him because their father loved Joseph more. Genesis 37:3 says, "Now Israel (Jacob) loved Joseph more than all his sons, because he was the son of his old age; and he made him a varicolored tunic." Verse 2 says of the brothers, "and so they hated him." Verse 5 says that after they heard his dream, "they hated him even more." Verse 8 says, "So they hated him even more for his dreams and for his words." Verse 11 speaks what we would expect, "And his brothers were jealous of him." Acts 7:9 confirms this when it says, "And the patriarchs became jealous of Joseph and sold him into Egypt. And yet God was with him."

When you are jealous over the attention or love shown to others, and not to you, it can lead to intense hatred for that person with whom you compare yourself. Jealousy is the desire to have the same thing for yourself that someone else has. There is another word in Greek (phthonos) that refers to the desire to deprive another person of what he has. It is often translated "envy." Jealousy is a serious problem, and can quickly destroy your joy and growth in the Lord.

One of my children needed some shelves in his room. He was so happy to get them. When my other son saw them, he said, "What about me? I need some shelves in my room, too!" My first thought was, "You should be glad to have your own room!'' But, I soon realized that we were on the verge of expressing jealousy over what someone else has that we don't have. It's natural to act that way. But, that's not the way God's *LOVE* responds. My child was concluding that because he did not receive any shelves for his room as his brother did, that meant that Dad did not love him as much. That's the ''Joseph problem'' all over again! I reassured him of my love, and also made plans about his need of shelves!

Jealousy in the lives of adults can be more damaging than the simple problems children encounter in growing up. Jealousy is serious whenever it occurs and should be dealt with immediately. But, adults have a tendency to harbor hatred and resentment much longer than children. One lady expressed to me the jealousy she had in her heart over the attention that a certain very attractive lady always received. In her sane moments she realized that people were responding in a very normal way to the other lady. She was beautiful, and she was very sweet and kind. People liked to be around her. The jealous lady was actually bitter toward God for not making her as pretty as the other lady. How foolish we all are, but how very normal! Our own worth and self-image is often affected by our comparison to others. Get that spirit of jealousy out of your heart as soon as possible. Learn to thank God for what He's done in your life, and learn to rejoice with the blessings bestowed upon others. It will do wonders for you!

Love does not brag

The King James Version reads, ''vaunteth not itself.'' The Greek word is used only here in I Corinthians 13:4. Clement of Alexandria (early church leader) says that it means to ornament oneself with emphasis on the extraneous and useless. God's *LOVE* does not brag about that which is unimportant and useless.

We often put the emphasis upon things that do not last and are not eternal. We brag about cars, clothes, trophies, awards, houses, boats, sports, etc. Jesus referred to this problem in Matthew 6:19-21:

> "Do not lay up for yourselves treasures upon earth, where moth and rust destroy, and where thieves break in and steal. But lay up for yourselves treasures in heaven, where neither moth nor rust destroys, and where thieves do not break in or steal; for where your treasure is, there will your heart be also."

The world is passing away says I John 2:17. We are told not to love it. We brought nothing into this world and it is certain that we will take nothing out of it (I Timothy 6:7). Those who refuse to brag are those who understand that everything we have comes from God. We are to be stewards of what He has given us. I Corinthians 4:7 asks the question, "And what do you have that you did not receive?"

I was in a friend's home admiring some trophies that he had won in various athletic contests. He seemed proud of them, and they were displayed in a place where everyone who walked into his house would automatically notice them. I asked him about their value. He laughed, and pointed to one of them that was already broken and was obviously a very cheap trophy. Those trophies were of no use to him, and with the passing of time, held little value in his life. He said that they reminded him of what is *not* important, and he was getting ready to throw them all away. They were useless, and what was the point in bragging about them? I agreed.

The sad thing about someone who brags over his achievements and accomplishments is that it has a tendency to drive others away, rather than closer to you. No one likes to be a friend to a braggart. It is irritating to listen to someone brag about unimportant things. It reveals a lack of love for people.

When you love with God's *LOVE*, you learn to "boast in the Lord," rather than yourself. Psalm 34:2 says, "My soul shall make its boast in the Lord; . . ." Psalm 44:8 adds, "In God we have boasted all day long, and we will give thanks to Thy name forever." I Corinthians 1:31 reminds us, ". . . Let him who boasts, boast in the Lord." A loving person learns to brag about Who God is and what God can do, rather than what *he* can do.

Bragging can become such a part of you that you don't discern that you are doing it. One example that affects me deals with the diplomas and degrees that I have achieved and have subsequently framed on beautiful plaques. For quite a long time I had them hanging in my office where everyone could see them. One day it struck me - what was the purpose of those plaques hanging in my office? Was it to impress people? Was I using them to make people respect me or respond to me? That did it! I removed the plaques. I felt 100% better about myself and my ministry. It was a little thing, but it was affecting me. What you are, you are. You don't have to impress people with plaques, trophies, degrees, etc. Everything we are and have comes from the Lord. To Him be all the glory! I don't want anything to stand in the way of loving people. I want to minister to people with a heart that boasts in the Lord, not myself. And, frankly, that's not easy to do!

Love is not arrogant

The King James Version says, ''is not puffed up.'' This verb is in the middle voice in Greek, which means that *LOVE* does not puff itself up. The only one who can make you arrogant is yourself!

Arrogance refers to the inflation of one's importance, abilities, or achievements. It seems closely related to the previous word - ''brag.'' Proverbs 27:2 says, ''Let another praise you, and not your own mouth; . . .''

The Pharisee was arrogant when he said, ''. . . God, I thank Thee that I am not like other people: swindlers, unjust, adulterers, or even like this tax-gatherer. I fast twice a week; I pay tithes of all that I get.'' (Luke 18:11-12).

I Corinthians 4:6-7 refers arrogance to a superior attitude. It's the attitude of the person who loses sight of the grace and sovereignty of God. When a person begins to think that his or her talents are self-produced, that person is arrogant. God gives us all our talents and opportunities.

There's nothing we have that we did not receive from Him.

You stop loving when you inflate your own importance. We often do that when we compare ourselves with others, which reveals a very insecure person! Arrogance depends upon constant evaluation with others. Arrogance seeks for people who are not quite as gifted or talented, and uses them as standards for evaluation. Arrogant people have a tendency to look down at other people. It is extremely difficult for an arrogant person to show love to others. It usually turns people off.

I realized the importance of this when I received a letter from one of the people who attend our church. This person heard me say as I was preaching, "Do you understand what I'm saying?" I didn't think too much about it, but this person felt it was an arrogant remark. It suggested that I knew more than the people did and that it was difficult for them to understand what I was saying. After careful evaluation of this person's criticism, I realized that my remark could be interpreted that way. I do not want to reflect that kind of attitude. I did a little heart-searching in an effort to root out arrogance that I might have felt. I Corinthians 8:1 does say, ". . . Knowledge makes arrogant, but love edifies." The context of that principle deals with the attitude of believers toward other believers who are weak in the faith and have serious doubts about some matters that others did not question. When we think we can do whatever we want to do even when other believers are hurt by our example, then we are arrogant, not loving!

Sometimes a non-loving person is spotted by the knowledge he or she displays. When you know what is right and wrong, but you become insensitive to the people around you who do not know what you do, you manifest a lack of love, and you appear arrogant.

Another form of arrogance happens when you tolerate sin. You begin to think that you do not have to obey God's standards. That's arrogance, and it keeps you from loving with God's *LOVE*. I Corinthians 5:2 is an illustration of this kind of arrogance. In the name of "love," many people commit sin or at least tolerate it. That love is false! Real love never violates God's Word. Although *LOVE* does not compromise with sin, it is always tender toward those who are struggling with sinful habits and practices. It always seeks to help, not hurt or hinder.

Love does not act unbecomingly

The root word here is our English word "scheme" or "schematic." It refers to the shape of something. The King James Version says, "does not behave itself unseemly." It comes to mean "tact." This word deals with etiquette. We would translate literally, "*LOVE* is not without shape."

I was greeting people after a church service when a young man crowded into the line and forced his presence upon me, insisting that what he had to say was more important than the others. He was rude and blunt. He was acting unbecomingly. His manner and words were without shape. *LOVE* is not rude. It says the proper thing at the proper time in the loving way. Many of us mean well, but we are not concerned with how it affects others. God's *LOVE* is concerned, and it shows in our relationships with others.

The verb translated "to act unbecomingly" is used in I Corinthians 7:36 where it says, "But if any man thinks that he is acting unbecomingly toward his virgin daughter, if she should be of full age, and if it must be so, let him do what he wishes, he does not sin; let her marry." This remark followed a discussion about the benefits of remaining single. This might lead some Christian fathers to believe that they would be doing the wrong thing if they gave their daughters in marriage. Paul corrects that possibility. The father was thinking that he would be acting "unbecomingly" or without shape toward his daughter if he let her marry when being single was of such great benefit to the Lord's work. The word "shape" might be better rendered, "plan." It was the plan of God with which the father was concerned. He did not want to be unloving toward his daughter, nor in his response toward God and His will.

The verb of I Corinthians 13:5 is used as a noun in I

Corinthians 12:23 when it refers to the "unseemly" members of the body of Christ. They are the rude and blunt ones - unloving in their response and deficient in tact and etiquette. The word is also used in Romans 1:27 referring to "indecent acts" committed by men involved sexually with other men. Such acts of immorality are "without shape," or "acting unbecomingly." God's *LOVE* does not act that way. It does not violate God's plan or will. In Revelation 16:15 we read, "Behold, I am coming like a thief. Blessed is the one who stays awake and keeps his garments, lest he walk about naked and men see his shame." The last word "shame" is from the same word "to act unbecomingly." To be naked reveals a lack of etiquette and proper morals (to say the least!).

From these usages of the word used in I Corinthians 13:5 we can piece together the idea behind the words "does not act unbecomingly." The "scheme" of things is based on the plan and will of God. The person who loves with God's *LOVE* is not without "scheme" or "plan." There is plenty of "shape" to what he says and does. God's *LOVE* is concerned about the way it is communicated to others as surely as what is communicated. It is important how you say something as well as what you say.

Laughing at a time of sorrow; rebuking when there's a need of encouragement; shouting when talking with only one person - all these responses are "without shape." They are rude, and lacking in kindness and proper timing. God's *LOVE* is much different!

Love does not seek its own

Literally, it reads "is not seeking the things of itself." The root problem here is obvious - selfishness! Philippians 2:3-4 says:

> "Do nothing from selfishness or empty conceit, but with humility of mind let each of you regard one another as more important than himself; do not merely look out for your own personal interests, but also for the interests of others."

God's *LOVE* is unselfish, humble, and sincerely interested

in others.

It's tragic when we see only what affects us. Many of us live in a world that shuts others out. We are self-centered. We talk about ourselves, and show interest only in what affects us. God's *LOVE* is greatly interested in other people. It has to - that's what it's like!

The words "does not seek" are in the present tense, indicating a continuous pattern. The self-centered person is continuously seeking things that affect himself only. The word "seeking" is also translated "zealous." Our idea of enthusiasm is based on this word. A selfish person is often enthusiastic about his selfishness - zealously pursuing those things in which the self is honored, promoted, or helped. Other people are rarely involved in the interests pursued. What is of interest to others is of no real concern to the selfish person. The selfish person sees others as a means to an end. The selfish person uses people to promote its own interests.

Matthew 20:28 says of our Lord, ". . . the Son of Man did not come to be served, but to serve, and to give His life a ransom for many." God's *LOVE* was evident in Jesus. He came for others, not Himself. Romans 15:2-3 points this out when it says, "Let each of us please his neighbor for his good, to his edification. For even Christ did not please Himself; . . ."

A father who comes home from work tired and faces his children's desires for his time and presence, is immediately confronted with the need for God's *LOVE* (and strength!). Shall he lie down for a few minutes and rest, or get up and play with his children? Will he be selfish or loving? Reading a paper or playing a game may determine a father's love!

Selfishness is often communicated at a young age when a child is not taught to share, but rather builds his life around the word "mine." Children who grow up receiving everything they could ever want or desire, often have problems of self-centeredness later in life. In athletics, one makes the choice of being the "star" or a "team player." The "star" (who also has athletic ability) is endured, accepted, and praised, until after the game. In the game of life, the "star" is not loving, but rather selfish. The "star" who uses others to get what he wants - popularity and fame - will soon discover that others will use him. The "team player" will develop concepts of sharing and ministering to others.

When marital partners build their response on self-gratification, the seeds of decay have already been planted in their marriage. No one likes to be used. No one cares to be around the self-centered person. Selfishness drives people away - it's not attractive, and it can never minister to your real needs. The husband who will not go shopping with his wife because he does not like it (when she loves it), is a selfish person. The wife who will not go with her husband to the ball game that he enjoys attending, but she hates, is also unloving and selfish.

The phrase "Do your own thing" has affected all of us in this modern culture, dominated by individual rights and demands. It is rooted in selfishness. We feel we have a right to do whatever we please, regardless of how it affects others. Our liberties become license to sin and hurt others. God's *LOVE* cares about the other person. It draws a line when the other person is left out. It considers the other person's view, and listens carefully. It tries hard to understand and to get excited over helping someone else.

Abraham demonstrated this unselfish *LOVE* of God when he said to his nephew, Lot (Genesis 13:9): "Is not the whole land before you? Please separate from me: if to the left, then I will go to the right; or if to the right, then I will go to the left." The selfish person would say, "As your uncle, I have a right to choose first. You can have what's left!"

David revealed an unselfish heart when he said, ". . . Far be it from me because of the Lord that I should do this thing to my lord, the Lord's anointed, to stretch out my hand against him, since he is the Lord's anointed." (I Samuel 24:6). From a human perspective, David could have been justified in killing Saul. But, he did not act selfishly. He waited on the plan and timing of God. He demonstrated concern for King Saul, in spite of what Saul had done to him.

Are you selfish? God's *LOVE* cannot seek the things that promote yourself. His *LOVE* forces you to be concerned and deeply interested in others.

Love is not provoked

It is somewhat of a mystery as to why the King James Version reads, "is not *easily* provoked." The word "easily" is not in the Greek text, and weakens the point. God's *LOVE* is never provoked! Not at all!

The Greek word translated "provoke" is from two words: "alongside of" and "to sharpen." God's *LOVE* is not made sharp by others. It does not get bitter by the reactions or attacks of others. The verb is also in the middle voice in Greek, meaning that it does not let itself get continually provoked. In other words, if you get provoked, it's your problem! You did it to yourself! It's easy to blame others or the circumstances around you.

As I write this particular page today, I am aware of a letter from a lady in our church who is "provoked" and "hurt" over the reactions of others to her ministry. She is not helping herself. She is wearing her heart on her sleeve! She is overly sensitive to what others say. She often evaluates meaningless incidents as personal attacks upon her character and ministry. What is the answer for her? A giant dose of God's *LOVE!* Her problem is a lack of God's *LOVE* in her life, the very thing that she accuses others of not having toward her.

It's right to get provoked at things and situations that are wrong. In Acts 17:16, we learn that Paul was provoked over the idolatry in the city of Athens. If you want to get "ticked off" at something, then get provoked over idolatry - it makes God mad also! But, it's never right to get provoked at people. Paul experienced that once in his relationship with Barnabas (Acts 15:39). It was a disagreement over John Mark going with them on their next missionary journey. Paul did not want to take him along in that he was a "dropout" from a previous missionary trip (Acts 13:13). Barnabas (son of encouragement) had a heart for him, as well as being a relative. Paul and Barnabas got provoked at one another, and it caused them to separate from each other. Regardless of your view as to whose fault it was, the real problem was a lack of God's *LOVE*. God's *LOVE* is never provoked at people, although it is often provoked at situations and practices that are wrong and sinful.

Consider the example of Christ (I Peter 2:23). When He was reviled, He did not revile in return. It's the opposite side of "loving your enemies (Matthew 5:38-48)." It's easy to get upset with people to the point of wanting a "pound of flesh." You want to get even with them. Sometimes this leads to a permanent barrier between you and that person who provoked you. That bitterness can eat your heart out!

Never seek revenge! Leave that to God (Romans 12:17-21). Be upset with things that are wrong, but don't let that carry over to the people who are involved. God's *LOVE* never gets provoked at people. After all, it is patient and kind!

One individual with whom I am acquainted in the ministry got very provoked one day at another pastor who from all appearances had attacked his credibility as a pastor. A deep breach occurred that day between these two men. It resulted in the man leaving the ministry, and today his bitterness continues. He has never forgiven the other man for what he said about him. Tragic!

Love does not take into account a wrong suffered

The King James Version reads, "thinketh no evil." The definite article in Greek is found in front of the word "evil." It refers to the particular evil which has made an attack on you. It is not referring to evil in general.

The great problem here is our ability to forgive. When we have been wronged, it is hard to forgive and forget. In modern Greek, the words "take into account" refer to an accountant. It means "to calculate." God's *LOVE* does not spend time "calculating" the evil done as to how to "get even" or "get revenge." It refuses to dwell on it.

Philippians 4:8 gives a list of things to think about (same word - to calculate) — things that are true, honorable, right, pure, lovely, and of good repute. These things are worthy of much thought. We are to let our minds dwell on these good things, not the wrong things done to us. The longer you live, the more aware you become of how futile it is to get revenge. You hurt yourself deeply when you do not forgive. People are people, and there will be times when they will wrong you. You must learn to live with that, and most of all, learn to forgive.

When someone you love does something wrong to you, it especially hurts. It's easy to remember it, and to let the wrong stand as a barrier to a deeper and more intimate relationship. It's hard to forgive, and doubly hard to forget. Many married couples have used the wrong of the past to hurt the other partner in the present. They are both hurt by this tactic, and little good ever comes of it. How much sweeter it is to forgive, bury it, and never bring it up again!

A Christian friend found himself "calculating" against his wife because of something she had done. Before they were married, she had been unfaithful to him during the time of their engagement. She had repented and sought forgiveness. He had said to her at the time that he would forgive her. Now, twenty years later, he used that incident to take revenge on something his wife had done. He hurt her deeply, as well as himself. As he said to me, "I don't know why I did that!" God's *LOVE* was not controlling him at the time, and when God's *LOVE* is not operating, we are all susceptible to saying and doing terrible things that hurt others.

When you let your mind concentrate on the wrong done to you, you will find a great deal of bitterness and resentment toward the person who did the wrong to you. Don't continue to think about it! Unless you have God's *LOVE* controlling you, your relationship with that person will be seriously damaged.

Romans 12:21 advises, "Do not be overcome by evil, but overcome evil with good." That's the proper way to handle it. Return good for evil. That's God's *LOVE* in action! When people see that kind of reaction, they'll find it hard to believe! There can be only one explanation - the control of God's Holy Spirit in that person's life!

One of the commonest ways that married couples reflect this problem is by refusing to give the love and affection that the other partner needs and desires - all because that partner did or said something that offended the other partner. That often leads to more serious problems. It is better to forgive - always! Seeking revenge or trying to get even has proven to me to be one gigantic waste of time! But, if I am not controlled by God's *LOVE*, my old sinful nature automatically tries to get even when I am wronged.

A friend in the ministry wrote me a nasty letter one day. What he said about me was not true. He was very religious and spiritual in how he said it, but it still hurt very deeply. I immediately wrote a letter back, answering the accusations and defending myself. I subtly began to accuse him of a failure to love. I said it so well, I was quite proud of myself. Several weeks later, the Lord convicted me of my attitude and my lack of love for that man. I quickly wrote him a letter, thanking him for what he had said, assuring him that the Lord had a purpose in it — that I had learned a great lesson through it — and I then expressed my love for him, that in spite of our disagreements, I deeply appreciated his ministry and his patience with me. It was such a joy to see how God used that to bind our hearts back together again! God's *LOVE* really works!

The hardest thing to admit is that you are wrong. Maybe the wrong done to you is really wrong, but your attitude toward that wrong can also be wrong! How we need God's *LOVE* and forgiveness! Think of what it would be like for all of us if God treated us with revenge for the ways in which we have wronged Him! Thanks be to God for His loving patience and continual forgiveness! We are so undeserving!

It helps me to express kindness and loving words to someone who has wronged me. (That isn't my natural inclination!) The next time that happens to you, try to say something kind or loving to the person who has wronged you. First, ask God to help you to say it with love, not revenge. You'll be amazed at the results! I think we would all get along much better if we just stop "calculating" over what others do to us! God's *LOVE* has no time for such calculation!

Love does not rejoice in unrighteousness, but rejoices with the truth

At the sight of evil and sin in others, God's *LOVE* automatically refrains from rejoicing. God's *LOVE* is saddened when hearing of the defeats and tragedies in other believers' lives. As I write this today, I'm reminded of a phone call telling me of one of my believing friends who has fallen into moral sin. My heart is sad and heavy. There are some who would be glad if they knew about this. They would say that he is getting what he deserves. But, that's not the way of God's *LOVE*.

It's easy to be glad at another's misfortune when it makes you look better. We sense a satisfaction within when our competition is defeated or even destroyed. That's rooted in an unloving attitude. God's *LOVE* rejoices with the truth, because the truth can set us free.

Gossip is frequently rooted in a lack of love for others. When we seem to take great pleasure in telling others about another person's faults, weaknesses, or sins, we reveal a lack of God's *LOVE*. God's *LOVE* refuses to be happy when hearing of unrighteousness. It resists a censorious spirit, or a judgmental attitude. It knows of God's grace and forgiveness. It believes in healing and restoration. It speaks the good about others, not the evil. III John 4 says, "I have no greater joy than this, to hear of my children walking in the truth."

One of the men in our ministry was known for his critical remarks of others. He often told others about people who had fallen into sin. He seemed to take pleasure in condemning them and saying things like "they got what they deserved." One day his wife shared with me his lack of love for her and their children. I should have known. God's *LOVE* would have been different in its response toward the sins of others than what this man continually reflected in his life. No wonder that his family did not sense his love for them! His unloving attitude toward others was evidence of his lack of God's *LOVE* in his own life.

I like what one dear lady friend of mine said when hearing of a mutual friend who had fallen into moral sin. She said, "I can't believe that of him . . . as a matter of fact, I won't believe it until I hear it from his own lips!" I liked the way she defended our mutual friend. She took no delight in hearing of his sin, but was rather grieved over the very mention of that possibility! I Peter 4:8 states, "Above all, keep fervent in your love for one another, because love covers a multitude of sins."

When God's *LOVE* controls you, there is a commitment to "the truth." So often people share things that others have told them and which they do not know firsthand. There is also the problem of how we share something. "The truth" is not always evident in the way people tell something. They may be telling the truth from their perspective, but it may not be the "real truth." We need to be careful about accepting what others say without having substantial confirmation of the facts. God's *LOVE* "rejoices with the truth." It wants the truth above anything else! It is not satisfied with mere hearsay. It does not tolerate gossip.

Summary - eight negatives

We have been studying what God's *LOVE* is not. It is not . . . (1) jealous, (2) bragging, (3) arrogant, (4) rude, (5) selfish, (6) provoked, (7) calculating revenge, (8) happy over the sins of others. These eight negatives reveal to us what God's *LOVE* refuses to do. These are natural tendencies with all of us. Without God's *LOVE* controlling our lives, these eight negatives will become positive attitudes and actions in all we do and say. They remind us of our need of the Holy Spirit's power and control.

How love reacts to circumstances | 6

". . . bears all things, believes all things, hopes all things, endures all things."

Four simple statements are in verse 7, but they're filled with practical advice. God's LOVE is expressed toward people, but it can also be seen by the way it reacts to the "all things" of life. Things do not always turn out the way we planned or expected (in case you hadn't noticed!). Changing circumstances are sometimes the barometer of our spiritual maturity. How do we react when things do not go the way we wanted?

The first thing we must do is to establish the fact that "all things" are a part of God's plan and will. Not everyone agrees with that. In order to help us adjust to the "things" we do not understand or especially appreciate, we usually resort to the opinion that God allows these "things" but that He certainly wouldn't cause them! But what does the Scripture say? Romans 8:28 says, "And we know that God causes all things to work together for good to those who love God, to those who are called according to His purpose." That verse insists that God is causing "all things." Romans 11:36 adds, "For from Him and through Him and to Him are all things. To Him be the glory forever. Amen." He is the source, channel, and object of everything! That's pretty clear, isn't it? Ephesians 1:11 says that He "works all things after the counsel of His will." That seems to indicate that He is not a passive observer to the events in our lives -

He is quite active as well as being quite purposeful in everything that happens.

We will not react properly to the changing circumstances of life until we recognize the sovereign control of God in all that happens. There is no such thing as "chance" or "coincidence" with God. Proverbs 16:33 puts it this way: "The lot is cast into the lap, but its every decision is from the Lord." How can we truly be thankful for everything (I Thessalonians 5:18) if we do not acknowledge it all as coming from the Lord? When we see things with design and purpose to them, we will be more grateful for them. Ephesians 5:20 says, "always giving thanks for all things in the name of our Lord Jesus Christ to God, even the Father." Revelation 4:11 reminds us of God's purpose and design behind the "all things" of our lives when it says:

> "Worthy art Thou, our Lord and our God, to receive glory and honor and power; for Thou didst create all things, and because of Thy will they existed, and were created."

God's Love reacts with protection

The first phrase of I Corinthians 13:7, "bears all things, . . ." is not referring to endurance, but rather to protection. The Greek word used here means "to cover" or "to protect." In modern Greek it refers to a "roof" of a house. God's *LOVE* puts up a shelter or roof. It keeps something off which might threaten. It's the same idea as in I Peter 4:8 when it says, ". . . love covers a multitude of sins."

Sometimes the "all things" we are to cover and protect are seen as threats to our own security. It's difficult under those circumstances to cover and protect. When your friend is exposed for some reason as being weak and sinful, what is your first reaction? To cover and protect? Or, is it to display publicly and let everyone know how bad he or she is? A loving friend is one to whom you can trust your character and reputation when you are out-of-town. There is no fear or insecurity when God's *LOVE* is present.

A beautiful example of the protecting, covering *LOVE*

of God is found in the story of Jonathan and David. I Samuel 18:1 tells us that "the soul of Jonathan was knit to the soul of David, and Jonathan loved him as himself." Later on, we read of how Saul (Jonathan's father) was plotting to kill David. In I Samuel 19:1-7, Jonathan's love is evident:

> "Now Saul told Jonathan his son and all his servants to put David to death. But Jonathan, Saul's son, greatly delighted in David. So Jonathan told David, saying 'Saul my father is seeking to put you to death. Now therefore, please be on guard in the morning, and stay in a secret place and hide yourself. And I will go out and stand beside my father in the field where you are, and I will speak with my father about you; if I find out anything, then I shall tell you.' Then Jonathan spoke well of David to Saul his father, and said to him, 'Do not let the king sin against his servant David, since he has not sinned against you, and since his deeds have been very beneficial to you. For he took his life in his hand and struck the Philistine, and the Lord brought about a great deliverance for all Israel; you saw it and rejoiced. Why then will you sin against innocent blood, by putting David to death without a cause?' And Saul listened to the voice of Jonathan, and Saul vowed, 'As the Lord lives, he shall not be put to death.' Then Jonathan called David, and Jonathan told him all these words. And Jonathan brought David to Saul, and he was in his presence as formerly."

What wonderful love Jonathan had for David! David returned the favor to Jonathan after his death. In II Samuel 9 we learn of how David took care of Mephibosheth, the son of Jonathan, for the rest of his life.

Yes, God's *LOVE* "covers" and protects those we love. It is not love when you inform others of how your friends have failed or sinned against God. It is not love when you do not prevent your friend from falling into danger, disaster, or embarrassment. It is not love when you do not defend your friend's character or reputation in his absence.

God's *LOVE* that "bears (covers) all things" in a marriage will not only provide financial security (a type of covering), but will quickly defend your marriage partner in the presence of others. God's *LOVE* will not give or allow remarks to be said about your partner that tear down instead of build up.

God's Love reacts with peace

The second phrase in I Corinthians 13:7, "believes all things," is not referring to the gullibility that often characterizes certain people. It's not saying that you check off your brains and never try to get the facts about anything, but instead simply believe whatever is told to you. That, of course, is ridiculous, and can get you into a great deal of trouble in your life.

This phrase speaks of a quiet confidence in everything that is happening. You know that it is for your good and God's glory. It is characterized by peace, not worry. Thanksgiving flows from the heart of one who "believes all things." There is the calm assurance that everything will be all right.

Romans 11:36 says, "For from Him and through Him and to Him are all things. To Him be the glory forever. Amen." Since He is the source, channel, and goal of everything, why worry? Romans 8:28 states, ". . . all things work together for good to those who love God . . ." That's either true or it isn't! Do you believe that? Paul said in Philippians 4:6-7:

> "Be anxious for nothing, but in everything by prayer and supplication with thanksgiving let your requests be made known to God. And the peace of God, which surpasses all comprehension, shall guard your hearts and your minds in Christ Jesus."

We don't always express thanks for things that happen - it's no wonder we find it hard to "believe all things," or to have peace in what is happening all around us. When God's *LOVE* controls, we can relax, and be confident that our sovereign God is doing all things well.

God's Love reacts with promise

The phrase "hopes all things" is characteristic of an optimistic heart. It is the quality of one who is continually looking to the future. It is the love that is based on what

God can do. Ephesians 3:20 says: "Now to Him who is able to do exceeding abundantly beyond all that we ask or think, according to the power that works within us." Nothing is too difficult for God, so the one who "hopes all things" sees the difference that a loving God can make. It never writes off anyone - it has hope!

God's *LOVE* is not pessimistic, but optimistic. It always hopes for the best. In a discussion one day with another Christian worker, we were evaluating a certain person's lifestyle. For many years, this person had proven to be a certain kind of person, and though there were repeated efforts to give him another chance, he continually failed to live up to the expectations of others. Another occasion had arisen which afforded this individual "another chance." Human nature and factual evidence told us to give up on him - love said otherwise. Fortunately, love overruled, and he was given another chance. To the amazement of all of us, he began to really produce for the Lord and his whole lifestyle changed! Thanks to love, things are different now in his life. A good lesson for all of us! Love is willing to risk for the benefit of others. Sometimes you have to "take a chance" when human reason says otherwise. Love does not give up easily.

The love that "hopes all things" is also aware of God's plan for the future. Things are going to get better - it's just a question of when! When the Lord Jesus comes back there are going to be some dramatic changes - praise God! The "all things" of life can look mighty discouraging at times, were it not for the sovereignty of God. God is working the "all things" for His glory and our good. We can relax and know that they will turn out for the best. We have nothing to fear in this regard. His love puts that fear out of our hearts and replaces it with a confidence - a solid hope, built on the character of God Himself.

God's Love reacts with patience

The *LOVE* that "endures all things" is the one that can stand the pressure when things are not going right. The word translated "endures" is from a Greek word meaning "to bear up under" or "to remain under." This word is different from the word in verse 4 where it says "love is patient." In I Cor. 13:4 it is a patience toward people (long-suffering). Here it is a patience toward things. God is never said to be in need of a patience toward things. He is controlling everything, so obviously He's not upset about anything!

Even after all human hope is gone, God's *LOVE* will patiently endure for Jesus' sake. I have seen this many times in the case of the terminally ill. When cancer afflicts the people of God, and all human hope is gone for possible recovery, and the words of the doctor reveal a certain limited period of time in which to live on this earth, that's a great opportunity for God's *LOVE* to take over! That *LOVE* of God can endure when everything else can't.

James tells us (James 1:2-4):

> "Consider it all joy, my brethren, when you encounter various trials, knowing that the testing of your faith produces endurance. And let endurance have its perfect result, that you may be perfect and complete, lacking in nothing."

God's *LOVE* can sustain you in the deepest trial and in the darkest night. Deuteronomy 33:27 says, "The eternal God is a dwelling place, and underneath are the everlasting arms; . . ." What wonderful security during the trials of life!

God's *LOVE* endures the circumstances of every day that produce impatience in most of us. We are impatient with the speed and quality of the work others do. God's *LOVE* endures. We are often impatient at the little inconveniences of life - traffic on the freeway, long lines at stores, offices, etc. - but God's *LOVE* changes the picture, and allows us to relax. God's *LOVE* concentrates on what is really important, and sees His gracious Hand behind everything that is happening in our lives.

Summary on "All things"

Let's face it - "all things" aren't always to our liking. It is one thing to believe intellectually that God is in control, it's quite another thing to relax emotionally in times of stress, when the "all things" are going a different direction than we had planned or hoped for.

Our reaction to circumstances is often a barometer of God's *LOVE*. When His *LOVE* controls, we relax more, and depend more upon Him. We recognize that things are always changing, and though we do not know how they will turn out, He does!

When you are handling "all things" correctly, there is a spirit of thankfulness (Eph. 5 :20; I Thess. 5:18) and joy in your heart. There is a certain peace governing your emotional response to things. People like being around you in times of pressure. You make them feel at ease and worthwhile. You seem to see the importance of what is happening for all concerned. You don't unleash your impatience at people - you're easy on them and loving to them. You're very protective and always defending the motives of those you love. Their character and reputation is in good hands when left with you.

We are wasting valuable time when we get so upset over changing circumstances. There is a purpose behind them (Ecclesiastes 3:1 ff) even when we are not aware of it. Have you ever had one of those days when nothing seemed to go right? That happened to me the other day. I was absolutely confused as to why God would allow things to develop as they had that particular day. But, in the midst of that "mess" (from my perspective, of course!) God led me to minister to a needy heart that would otherwise (if the "mess" had not occurred) had not happened. During this time, I could not understand what was happening, but when it was all over, I once again saw the loving hand of God behind it all.

May God give us His perspective of what is happening. He is in control, and His *LOVE* can control us in "all things."

Pursue

Love

IT'S YOUR GREATEST NEED

FIRST CORINTHIANS 13

PART THREE

LOVE IS GREATER THAN ALL THE GIFTS . . .

1. It is greater in future endurance.
   I Corinthians 13:8-12

2. It is greater in present experience.
   I Corinthians 13:13

7 | Love never fails

"Love never fails; but if there are gifts of prophecy, they will be done away; if there are tongues, they will cease; if there is knowledge, it will be done away. For we know in part, and we prophesy in part; but when the perfect comes, the partial will be done away. When I was a child, I used to speak as a child, think as a child, reason as a child; when I became a man, I did away with childish things. For now we see in a mirror dimly, but then face to face; now I know in part, but then I shall know fully just as I also have been fully known."

- I Corinthians 13:8-12

Gifts, as wonderful as they are, will not last forever . . . love will! The desire for spiritual gifts is proper (I Corinthians 14:1), but not the highest pursuit of the believer. Next to glorifying God (I Corinthians 10:31), and no doubt reflecting it, is to love God, and others. Jesus said to a lawyer who asked about the greatest commandment of all, "You shall love the Lord your God with all your heart, and with all your soul, and with all your mind." Jesus said that this was the greatest commandment of all, and that the second greatest was just like it - "You shall love your neighbor as yourself." Yes, God's *LOVE* is the greatest!

Spiritual gifts are greatly misunderstood and abused. They are wonderful blessings when God's *LOVE* is controlling, but they can become "curses" when His *LOVE* is absent! *LOVE* is more important than spiritual gifts, but it takes a measure of maturity and growth to know why.

The key phrase to this section of Scripture (I Corinthians 13:8-12) is "love never fails." The Greek would read literally, "the love never at any point of time is failing." It never fails to be effective or to accomplish things. It never lacks force or power. It always works! Other good things (like spiritual gifts) can fail, both in time and under certain circumstances. God's *LOVE* never fails! We need it more than anything else in our lives.

1. The inability of certain gifts to last forever

To illustrate the unfailing nature of love and its absolute importance to our lives and ministries, the apostle Paul reveals the temporary nature of certain gifts. He mentions three gifts or the results of three gifts in verse 8.

> "If there are gifts of **prophecy**, they will be done away; if there are **tongues**, they will cease; if there is **knowledge**, it will be done away."

The word "if" (eite - Greek) can be translated, "if at this point in time, and it is so." In other words, there is no doubt about the existence of these gifts. The word "if" is a class condition in Greek that refers to that which is true. We might use the English word "since." We could translate "Since at this point in time there are prophecies . . ." At the writing of I Corinthians (around 50-52 A.D.), the gifts of prophecy, tongues, and knowledge, were definitely in operation.

When commenting on prophecy and knowledge, Paul uses the same phrase - "will be done away." The word "prophecy" is in the plural, and should be translated "prophecies." It is referring to content, not proclamation. The result of the gift of prophecy is "prophecies." The word "knowledge" is, of course, in the singular as it always is (no such word as "knowledges"!). The phrase "will be done away" suggests a phasing out over a period of time. It can be translated "to render inoperative" or "to become ineffective." At the writing of I Corinthians, they (prophecies and knowledge) were serving an important purpose, but something better was coming which would eliminate the need for them.

When Paul refers to "tongues" he changes the verb from "will be done away," to "they will cease." Tongues will come to an abrupt stop. Prophecies and knowledge will be replaced by something better; tongues will not be replaced. They will cease to be needed because of what is coming. Tongues were needed as long as the prophecies and knowledge were still communicated. Prophecies and knowledge are both referring to revelation from God. At the time of I Corinthians (one of the first of the epistles of Paul), the "revelation" of New Testament truth was incomplete. A portion of what the New Testament now contains had been put into writing by the time Paul wrote this letter to Corinth. There was a great deal more to follow, much of which would be revealed by the apostle Paul (as well of John, James, Jude, and Peter). Tongues were necessary until the time when "prophecies" and "knowledge" would be phased out.

If you read I Corinthians 13:8 carefully, you discover that the point in time at which "prophecies" and "knowledge" will be phased out is the same time at which "tongues" will cease to exist. Naturally, the great debate is over the point in time when this would occur! If "tongues" are still in operation today, then "prophecies" and "knowledge" are still being communicated to men. That is a dangerous position! Can we add new revelation to what is contained in the 66 books of the Bible? Many cultic groups believe so, and that is why they have additional revelation which they treat with equal honor and respect as the Bible itself.

The purpose of "tongues" according to I Corinthians 14:22, is that they are "for a sign, not to those who believe, but to unbelievers." In I Corinthians 14:21 we have a quotation from Isaiah 28:11. The people of Israel were not responding to God's revelation, and God used "tongues" (the language of the Assyrians who would bring God's judgment upon them - which happened in 722 B.C.) to confirm the authority and accuracy of His revelation to them through the prophets.

Jesus said in Mark 16:17-20 that "tongues" were a part of those "signs" God would use to "confirm the word (v. 20)." Hebrews 2:1-4 says the same thing. We cannot escape the judgment of God if we reject His Word. That passage tells us that God's Word was spoken first by the Lord, and then it was "confirmed (same word as Mark 16:20)" unto us by "*those* who heard, God also bearing witness with *them*, both by signs and wonders and by various miracles and by gifts of the Holy Spirit according to His own will." The "those" and "them" are the apostles to whom God directly communicated New Testament truth. Their message was "confirmed (legal term - to authenticate as being genuine)" by miraculous signs, gifts of the Spirit. II Corinthians 12:12 concurs with this when it says that "the signs of a true apostle were performed among you with all perseverance, by signs and wonders and miracles."

As long as God was giving new revelation through His apostles and prophets (cf. Ephesians 2:20 and 3:5), "tongues" were needed to authenticate them and their message. These gifts, prophecies, knowledge, and tongues, were temporary. A point in time was coming in which they would no longer be needed. A point in time was coming when God's revelation would be finished . . . completed!

Two reasons are given as to why these gifts will not be permanent: (1) *Because they give only partial understanding* - I Cor. 13:9, "For we know in part, and we prophesy in part." Paul realized that he (in spite of the abundance of revelation given to him) did not have the complete truth; he had only partial understanding. As he wrote I Corinthians, it was not complete - there was more coming. (2) *Because something is coming that will bring complete understanding* - I Cor. 13:10, "But when the perfect comes, the partial will be done away." The word "comes" (aorist subjective) indicates a particular point in time. What is coming is described as "the perfect." What is meant by "the perfect?" This

Greek word is used in its various forms about 75 times in the New Testament. In all these passages, you will find about four major ideas in the usage of this word "perfect."

First, *It is used of that which is whole or complete.* It means that nothing is left out. It refers to sacrifices that are without blemish. God's *LOVE* is called "perfect" in I John 4:18. Perfect love doesn't lack anything. In that passage, it does not have room for fear. In Matthew 5:48 we are told to be "perfect" as our heavenly Father is. It is referring to the matter of loving our enemies. In order for us to be complete or total in our love, we must love our enemies, as well as our friends.

Secondly, *It is used for maturity.* The Greek philosophers (like Plato and Aristotle) used it when referring to the end of the learning process. It meant that there was no need for further advancement. The Bible uses it in this way in Colossians 1:28:

> "And we proclaim Him, admonishing every man and teaching every man with all wisdom, that we may present every man **complete** in Christ."

Thirdly, *It is used for biological growth.* Closely related to maturity, this usage refers to that which is "full-grown." In the case of people, it is the word for "adults." It is used of animals and humans, and is the opposite of children and youth. Adults capable of reproduction are "perfect," or full-grown. I Corinthians 14:20 uses this concept when it says, "Brethren, do not be children in your thinking; yet in evil be babes, but in your thinking be *mature.*"

Lastly, *It is used of completing a task.* In Acts 20:24, Paul spoke about his desire to "*finish* my course." He wanted to be faithful to God in fulfilling God's purpose for his life. Jesus used the word in John 4:34 when He said He wanted to "*accomplish* His (God the Father) work." He used it again in John 17:4 when He said, "I glorified Thee on the earth, having *accomplished* the work which Thou hast given Me to do." It is also used in John 19:28 when it says, "After this, Jesus, knowing that all things had already been *accomplished* . . ." II Chronicles 8:16 uses the word in the Greek translation of the Old Testament (the Septuagint) when it says, ". . . So the house of the Lord was *completed*."

Whatever "the perfect" is, it is the same in nature or substance as that which is called "in part." The partial is a part of the perfect, or the completed thing. That which is partial is described in verse 9 as being knowledge and prophecy. They are referring to God's revelation. Can we not then conclude that "the perfect" is also referring to God's revelation? The "perfect" thing that is coming is the completion of God's revelation to man. When it comes, the gifts that have given us new revelation from God would be phased out. They were continually being phased out with the writing of each New Testament book. The process would be completed with the writing of the final New Testament book. Which brings us to the main problem: Is the Bible in its 66 books a complete and final revelation from God? My answer is an emphatic "YES!" The gift of "tongues" would cease the moment this "perfect" thing would be here. If the "perfect" thing is referring to the completion of the New Testament, then the Biblical gift of tongues would cease to exist at that point.

How do we know that the Bible is a complete and final revelation from God? Jude 3 indicates that the point in time of God's revelation being spoken to man had already come:

> "Beloved, while I was making every effort to write you about our common salvation, I felt the necessity to write to you appealing that you contend earnestly for the faith which was once for all delivered to the saints."

But, how would we know that the last book in the process would be here? Would there always be a problem in church history of additional books? Should we be looking for that final book, or is it already here? The answer is found in the last book of the Bible, the Revelation, chapter 22 (the last chapter), verses 18-19:

> "I testify to everyone who hears the words of the prophecy of this book; if anyone adds to them, God shall add to him the plagues which are written in this book; and if anyone takes away from the words of the

> book of this prophecy, God shall take away his part from the tree of life and from the holy city, which are written in this book."

Some people argue that Revelation 22:18-19 is only to be applied to the book of Revelation, and not to the entire Bible. However, consider for a moment the contents of the book of Revelation. They deal with future events (at least from chapter four on) all the way into the eternal state. How can you add anything to that? All that God will do in the future has been recorded. No one can add to it, or take away from it without experiencing serious consequences!

The "perfect" thing that will come is the completed Bible. James 1:22-25 concurs with that view:

> "But prove yourselves doers of the word, and not merely hearers who delude themselves. For if any one is a hearer of the word and not a doer, he is like a man who looks at his natural face in a mirror; for once he has looked at himself and gone away, he has immediately forgotten what kind of person he was. But one who looks intently at the **perfect law**, the law of liberty, and abides by it, not having become a forgetful hearer but an effectual doer, this man shall be blessed in what he does."

The usage of the "mirror" as an illustration reminds us of I Corinthians 13:12. The word "perfect" is also used in James 1:25 as an adjective modifying the word "law," obviously referring to God's Word. God's Word is complete. Psalm 119:89 reminds us, "Forever, O Lord, Thy word is settled in heaven." God's revelation (as to its final and complete form communicated to man) was settled long ago in heaven before it was ever given to man. If God did not want to put a stamp of finality on His written Word, He easily could have eliminated Revelation 22:18-19!

As wonderful as God's revelation (the "perfect" thing) is, and as marvelous as the gifts for communicating it are (prophecy, knowledge, tongues), *LOVE* is greater because it will never fail!

We are glad for everyone who discovers spiritual gifts and uses them for the glory of God and the building up of

His Church. But, never forget that *LOVE* is greater. *LOVE* is eternal - it never fails! Gifts are temporary (regardless of your viewpoint as to how long they will be needed!). In all of your effort to discover your spiritual gifts, do not neglect God's *LOVE*. It is more important than using your gifts. Without God's *LOVE*, your spiritual gifts are ineffective in the building up of every believer. God's *LOVE* is what builds up (cf. Ephesians 4:16).

2. The illustration as to why things don't last forever

"When I was a child, I used to speak as a child, think as a child, reason as a child; when I became a man, I did away with childish things."

- I Corinthians 13:11

Why do things not last forever? Because we grow up! The words "did away with" are the same words as in verses 8 and 10. The "things" of the child could refer to prophecies and knowledge, that which is "partial" and not "perfect." They are lacking in complete understanding, like the child (Greek - nepios - one without speech, used normally of toddlers).

God's *LOVE* is the way of maturity. Knowledge, understanding, spiritual gifts, etc., can be reflective of immaturity, especially when God's *LOVE* is absent. The "perfect" thing (God's complete revelation) gives us understanding about God's *LOVE* and God's ways that produce a mature, loving lifestyle. God's *LOVE* never fails; spiritual gifts will run their course - they are temporary.

Some Bible teachers believe that the "perfect" thing is *LOVE* itself. There is reason for this from I John 4:18 where the word "perfect" is applied to the word "*LOVE*." However, the "perfect" thing in I Corinthians 13:10 had not arrived yet (at least at the time of the writing of I Corinthians - 50-52 A.D.). God's *LOVE* was certainly available at that time.

Some teachers insist that the "perfect" thing refers to

Jesus Christ at His second coming. They are especially influenced by the phrase in verse 12, "face to face." (Perhaps the words of the song, "Face to Face with Christ my Saviour," affects this!) But the adjective "perfect" in verse 10 is a neuter gender. It seems that if it were to be applied to Jesus Christ, it would appear in the masculine gender.

Others believe that the word "perfect" applies to the event of Christ's second coming, or to the future millennial age, or the eternal state. There is a lack of evidence for these views although we certainly have a right to state them as possible viewpoints.

A few have argued that the word "perfect" applies to the universal body of Christ. I Corinthians 12 does deal with the principles of body life. The gifts then would continue until the body of Christ is completed, obviously at the end of the age.

Some say that the word "perfect" refers to Paul's usage in Ephesians 4:13 where he says all the believers should attain to a ". . . mature man, to the measure of the stature which belongs to the fulness of Christ." This view argues that the "perfect" refers to maturity, and that seems to be supported by the illustration of I Corinthians 13:11 - ". . . when I became a man, I did away with childish things." The problem here is in determining whether that maturity is the maturity of the individual or of the corporate body of believers, and if so, when can we say that "maturity" has come?

In spite of the good points favoring each of these views of the "perfect" thing, it still seems to this writer that the best and most consistent view with other Scripture, is that the "perfect" refers to God's complete revelation in written form - namely, the Bible. Its obvious identification with the partial (prophecies and knowledge) seems to give strong support to this view. Also, the usage of the "mirror" in verse 12 is connected with other passages dealing with the Word of God (II Corinthians 3:18; James 1:22-25). The word "perfect" is also used of God's Word in James 1:25.

3. The instruction concerning their present understanding as contrasted with their future understanding

"For now we see in a mirror dimly, but then face to face; now I know in part, but then I shall know fully just as I also have been fully known."
- I Corinthians 13:12

The tendency of the Corinthians was spiritual pride over their knowledge (I Corinthians 8:1) and their gifts (I Corinthians 12). Paul's argument in chapter 13 is that the gifts are temporary, and that their present knowledge was incomplete - there was more coming than what they presently had available to them. They were pursuing the wrong things - knowledge and gifts. I Corinthians 14:1 tells the Corinthians to "pursue love." Desiring (being enthusiastic or zealous) spiritual gifts was fine, especially when they knew the importance of certain gifts (like prophecy), but God's *LOVE* was the greatest thing of all. It never fails. Their present knowledge was incomplete, and their usage of gifts would not last, but God's *LOVE* was permanent and eternal!

One day a young man with a great desire to teach God's Word came into my office to talk with me. He had many talents, and was a good student of God's Word. His ability to teach at his age was far superior to mine when I was his age. I marvelled at his gift and his understanding. He had a problem. People were not responding to his teaching. He asked why. I asked him, "Do you love the people you are teaching?" He was taken back by the question, and spent a few moments reflecting on it. Showing why he is going to be used of God in a great way, he said, "Thanks. I needed that reminder. Without love, we are nothing." He was teachable. I learned a great lesson from him on that score!

No matter how great your gifts, without God's *LOVE* you will fail. *LOVE* never fails! Paul said two things about the present understanding of the Corinthians: First, "Now we see in a mirror dimly." Second, "Now I know in part."

The usage of the word "mirror" appears only here and in James 1:25. The word "dimly" (ainigmati - English word "enigma" comes from this Greek word) means "in obscurity." Things are now like riddles, according to Paul. We don't see everything properly or correctly. Numbers 12:8 uses the word in the Greek Old Testament, when it says, "With him (Moses) I speak mouth to mouth, even openly, and not in *dark sayings* . . ." The Lord said that He would make Himself known to Moses. There would be no obscurity in his communication with Moses. At the time Paul wrote I Corinthians, the knowledge they had was often "obscure." It was not completely clear.

The second thing Paul said was "now I know in part." The partial knowledge he had was tremendous in comparison to the Corinthians, but Paul's knowledge was still not complete. It would be many years after his death that God would finally bring to an end His revelation to man (about 95 A.D. - John wrote "Revelation").

No matter what you know or you do not know, without God's *LOVE*, you will not be effective in ministry to others. Today we have a complete written revelation from God to man to study. But the need for God's *LOVE* is just as strong in our lives today as it was when Paul wrote I Corinthians! God's *LOVE* will continue forever. There is always room to grow in understanding and experiencing the *LOVE* of God.

Two of the staff members who work with me were not getting along. A particular issue that seemed minor to others was very important to both of them. They are not young men starting out in the ministry. Both have years and experience behind them. They saw this particular issue in two different ways. Each felt he was right and the other person wrong. Neither of them wanted to give in. Both assured me that they loved each other, but that this issue had to be settled. The problem was that the issue was of such a nature that a moral verdict as to who was right and who was wrong was totally impossible. There was no chapter and verse to point to. Instead, I appealed to them to love each other no matter what happened. They insisted that they did love each other, but still would not give in. It took quite a while to convince them from the Word of God that "giving in" could be a demonstration of God's *LOVE*! The whole thing seemed bigger than what it was. But, I once again saw that God was teaching them and myself a little more about His *LOVE* than any of us had encountered before.

We will not always know everything we would like to know, nor settle matters that we would like to settle. But, we can always experience and exercise a little more of God's *LOVE*. There are some things that we will never understand until we get to heaven! (There are no doubt some things that we will never know about God even after we do get to heaven - His greatness is "past finding out!")

Two things are said about the future understanding of the Corinthians. First, "Then face to face," secondly, "Then I shall know fully just as I also have been fully known." The "face to face" phrase could refer to being in heaven and seeing the Lord "face to face." Our knowledge then will certainly be superior to what it is now! However, this phrase could also be referring to the complete revelation in written form - "the perfect" thing that is coming, and now (today) has come! Verse 10 says, "*when* the perfect comes," and verse 12 says, "*then* face to face." This phrase should be connected with the word "mirror." "Face to face" is how we look into a "mirror." At the time of writing I Corinthians, things were not clear. They saw in the "mirror dimly." But when the entire New Testament would be completed, they would see clearly, or "face to face." In Genesis 32:30, Jacob says, ". . . I have seen God face to face . . ." Yet, Jesus said in John 1:18, "No man has seen God at any time; . . ." Jacob did have some direct knowledge about God, but he, as a mere man, could not see God. The finite could not comprehend the infinite. In Judges 6:22 Gideon said, ". . . For now I have seen the angel of the Lord face to face." He was not convinced of that fact until he saw him perform a miracle in his presence. He saw him before as a mere man, but his knowledge greatly increased when he saw the miracle.

Perhaps the best explanation of the phrase "face to face" is found in Numbers 12:6-8. The text says that ". . . he beholds the form of the Lord. . . ," and that God speaks to Moses ". . . mouth to mouth. . ." The knowledge and understanding of Moses is being contrasted with the knowledge of other prophets to whom God would speak ". . . in a vision . . ." or ". . . in a dream" (v.6). This text seems to be the one Paul might have had in mind when he was writing I Corinthians 13:12.

The phrase ". . . but then I shall know fully just as I also have been fully known." could refer to being in heaven with the Lord, or again, it could refer to God's complete revelation in written form. A complete, full understanding of the plan of God is found in the Scriptures. It was not complete when I Corinthians was written, but by the end of the first century A.D., it was. The words, "just as I also have been fully known," (aorist passive form in Greek) refer to God's knowledge of him in terms of his salvation. Paul's knowledge would be brought up to that particular level of understanding when the Word of God was completed. Naturally, there will be much more to learn in eternity! Even those who believe that this full knowledge is not the written Word of God, but future heavenly knowledge, will admit that we will continue to learn and to know things forever and ever!

Though many views have been given on these verses in I Corinthians 13:8-12, one thing remains clear to all - God's *LOVE* will not fail! When certain gifts are no longer needed, and knowledge is finally complete, God's *LOVE* will still be there - still needed! Your greatest need is still God's *LOVE*, and always will be.

Love is now! | 8

"But now abide faith, hope, love, these three; but the greatest of these is love."
- I Corinthians 13:13

God's *LOVE* is greater than all the spiritual gifts that the Holy Spirit has given to the believers! It is greater in future endurance, and it is also greater in present experience. God's *LOVE* is now! The words, "But now abide" are present tense in Greek. It means that God's *LOVE* constantly, continually abides. Along with *LOVE*, two other things continue to abide: faith and hope; but, *LOVE* is the greatest!

When my oldest son was just a little boy, I invited him to jump off our backyard fence into my arms. He hesitated and said he was afraid. I said, "Don't you believe that Daddy can catch you?" He said he believed me. I think he hoped that I would make good on my promise, even though he suspected the possibility of error! Finally, I said, "Do you believe that Dad loves you very much?" At that point, he jumped! Fortunately I caught him. My love for him persuaded him to trust me. Faith and hope are important, but love is greater and stronger.

My faith in the Lord is questionable at times, but His *LOVE* for me never is! My hope in Him is "shaky" at times, but I am absolutely secure in His *LOVE*. Salvation is not based upon my ability to believe; it is based on a loving God Who *LOVES* me even though He knows what I am like. His

LOVE has granted me total forgiveness because of what His Son did for me at the cross. John 3:16 puts it beautifully: "For God so loved the world that He gave His only begotten Son, that whoever believes in Him should not perish, but have eternal life." God's *LOVE* is so strong. Solomon wrote in Song of Solomon 8:6-7:

> "Put me like a seal over your heart, like a seal on your arm. For love is as strong as death, jealousy is as severe as Sheol; Its flashes are flashes of fire, the very flame of the Lord. Many waters cannot quench love, nor will rivers overflow it; If a man were to give all the riches of his house for love, it would be utterly despised."

The Lord reminded the nation of Israel of His great *LOVE* for them, when He said through Moses in Deuteronomy 7:6-9:

> "For you are a holy people to the Lord your God; the Lord your God has chosen you to be a people for His own possession out of all the peoples who are on the face of the earth. The Lord did not set His love on you nor choose you because you were more in number than any of the peoples, for you were the fewest of all peoples, but **because the Lord loved you** and kept the oath which He swore to your forefathers, the Lord brought you out by a mighty hand, and redeemed you from the house of slavery, from the hand of Pharaoh king of Egypt. Know therefore that the Lord your God, He is God, the faithful God, who keeps His covenant and His lovingkindness to a thousandth generation with those who love Him and keep His command-ments."

It is God's great *LOVE* that brings security to the believer. It removes all doubts; it strengthens our faith; it encourages our hope and trust in His promises. It's because of His *LOVE* for us that we have any degree of confidence. I John 4:17-19 says:

> "By this, love is perfected with us, that we may have confidence in the day of judgment; because as He is, so also are we in this world. There is no fear in love; but perfect love casts out fear, because fear involves punishment, and the one who fears is not perfected in love. We love, because He first loved us."

We cannot explain our salvation on our personal worthiness or dedicated efforts to do what is right. We cannot earn nor do we deserve our salvation from sin, death, and Hell. There is only one explanation: "God so loved the world!" Ephesians 2:4 says, "But God, being rich in mercy, *because of His great love* with which He loved us." That's the only sufficient answer! God's *LOVE* is truly the greatest!

1. What faith, hope, and love have in common

A fascinating little problem is found in the Greek text of I Corinthians 13:13. The word "abide" is in the singular form, rather than the plural. One would expect the plural in that three things are mentioned that abide - faith, hope, and love.

One possible solution is that the writer expects the reader to supply the word "abide" after each of the three qualities in that verse. Faith abides, hope abides, and love abides. However, the phrase that ends the first statement, "these three," seems to point to a relationship between the three qualities, rather than viewing them separately. The writer seems to suggest that all three belong together - they have something in common - they are treated as one. It is one thing that continues to abide, and it is best described by three words: faith, hope, and love.

These three qualities are seen together in Romans 5:1-5. *Faith* is mentioned in verses one and two; *hope*, in verses four and five; and *love*, in verse five. In Colossians 1:4-5 we find all three together once again. It says, "Since we heard of your *faith* in Christ Jesus and the *love* which you have for all the saints; because of the *hope* laid up for you in heaven, of which you previously heard in the word of truth, the gospel." In some degree of closeness, we see the three mentioned in Ephesians 1:15-18. In verse 15 both *faith* and *love* are mentioned, and in verse 18 "the *hope* of his calling." One of the great texts using all three is found in I Thessalonians 1:3, where we read:

> "Constantly bearing in mind your work of **faith** and labor of **love** and steadfastness of **hope** in our Lord Jesus Christ in the presence of our God and Father."

Out of all the gifts, attributes, and resources available to the believer, nothing so characterizes what is really important and eternal as do those three words, faith, hope, and love. Every other attribute, attitude, and action somehow flows out of those three. Those three qualities describe the total of what God wants for us and has for us. Everything seems simple and clear when described by those three words. They can only flow out of a regenerated heart, one that has received a new nature from God. In man's natural state, he does not have those three qualities flowing out of his life. Only God can give us faith, hope, and love!

What do faith, hope, and love have in common? Consider the following three points:

First, *All three are the result of God's work in the heart of the believer.* Apart from divine intervention, man in his natural state is incapable of experiencing either faith, hope, or love. Man is described as being "dead in trespasses and sins (Ephesians 2:1)." Being spiritually dead, he is unable to respond with faith, hope, or love. He must be born again by the Spirit of God! Only then can he have true faith, hope, and love. Faith and love are stated to be "fruit" of the Holy Spirit in Galatians 5:22-23, and in that text, the word "hope" could be inserted as part of what joy, peace, and patience are all about.

Second, *All three describe the maturity which God desires in the life of every believer.* The Corinthians were immature (I Cor. 14:20) and fleshly (I Cor. 3:3). Their spiritual pride kept them from discovering true maturity in the Lord (as it does to many people today!). Faith, hope, and love were better qualities than what they were manifesting in their lives. If you want to describe maturity from God's viewpoint, then use God's words: faith, hope, and love. They tell it all. Nothing is left out.

Third, *All three are eternal and will be found in heaven as well as on earth.* Many commentators have tried to show the greatness of love over faith and hope by saying that faith and hope will no longer be needed when we get to heaven. They say, "Faith will be turned into sight, and hope will finally be realized." Heaven appears to be the end of faith and hope as far as the believer is concerned. But the Bible does not teach that. It is true that II Corinthians 5:7 says, "for we walk by faith, not by sight." But that does not say that we will not need faith when we get to heaven. On the contrary, Hebrews 11:6 says, ". . . without faith it is impossible to please . . ." God. There will be more reasons in heaven to have faith in God than we have now! Dependency and trust upon our living God will be greater then than now!

The more I grow in my knowledge of God, the greater is my faith and trust in Him. How much better it will be when I get to heaven! I will know more than I do now, and although my knowledge of God will eternally remain incomplete, the things I continue to discover about Him in eternity, will only increase my faith and confidence in Him! Heaven will be a wonderful place as we continue to discover and learn more and more about our wonderful Lord! Our faith will grow as our knowledge of Him increases, just like it does now! We will not be sitting upon clouds doing nothing! Heaven is not the end, but only the beginning of faith!

Hope is the anticipation of things promised. In heaven, hope will become more exciting. Realization and anticipation of God's promises and blessings will be lifted to new heights! We will not automatically see and know everything there is to know when we get to heaven. We will continue to learn and grow in our understanding and experience. Our hope will expand as we realize the infinite resources and possibilities we have available to us because an infinite God can make them possible. Revelation 21:5 says, ". . . Behold, I am making all things new . . ." Praise God!

Just as love continues to grow on earth, so it will increase continually in heaven. ". . . God is love." says I John 4:8, and ". . . love is from (out of) God; . . ." according to verse 7. Since God is infinite, it is obvious that the depth of love will never be discovered! We will continue to learn about God's *LOVE!* Romans 11:33 says, "Oh, the depth of the riches both of the wisdom and knowledge of God! How unsearchable are His judgments and unfathomable His ways!"

I'm so glad that God's *LOVE* continues to grow and expand in my life. The love I had for my wife when we got married was a wonderful thing. I'll never forget how I felt when I saw her come down that church aisle the night of our marriage - Wow! The excitement of that moment; the anticipation of what our love would mean to both of us in the days ahead; the thrill of committing ourselves to one another in marital love - what a moment that was! But, friends, it was nothing when compared to what we experience today! Our love has grown and deepened through the years. Sometimes I wonder how it could get any better, but then it does, and it always will! That's why statements about falling in and out of love seem so immature. Love grows and deepens over the years. It is not merely a momentary feeling of emotion - it's a lifetime of caring and sharing! We've had our share of problems, heartaches, and tears. But love has made them all worthwhile! God's *LOVE* is what we needed when we began our marriage, and it is what we need today more than ever before! It is also what we all will continue to need in heaven forever and ever!

2. Why love is greater than faith and hope

Faith, hope, and love are present in our lives now, and will be throughout eternity. But, the interesting and featured point of I Corinthians 13:13 is the statement, ". . . but the greatest of these is love." Why is that so? Faith and hope are certainly great and very needed. Why is love more important? What can it do that faith and hope cannot?

It is on the basis of this last phrase in I Corinthians 13 that I have (without hesitation) subtitled this book, *"The Greatest Need in Your Life."* God's *LOVE* is the greatest, but the question remains, "Why?" If God's *LOVE* is really the greatest, then it's no wonder why I Corinthians 14 begins with these words, "Pursue love." We ought to go after it with all our energies! We must give time to this pursuit, and determine to have God's *LOVE* above all else! Is that how you feel? Is that what you want? Is that what you understand to be your greatest need? If so, what are you doing about it? Are your priorities at the present time reflecting your pursuit of love? What time have you given today to cultivating this most important quality in your life? Is it really number one with you? Do you really want it more than you want financial reward or success? Do you really prefer God's *LOVE* to personal pleasure?

(1) *Love is greater than faith and hope because God is love.* God is not merely love, for He is that and much more. It is not correct to say "love is God," for that makes God an emotion and brings Him down to a human level. God is loving, but that doesn't say it all either. I John 4:8 says, ". . . God is love." The essence of His being and character, the motivation of His acts, the basis for all His relationships to man, is love. His love does not exclude His holiness or His righteousness. His love does not overlook or excuse sin. His love does not eliminate judgment or Hell. His love is perfect in every way, and very much different from the natural tendency of man and woman.

The Bible does *not* say, "God is faith" or "God is hope." He gives us faith and hope, but it is only of love that the Bible declares "God is." Therefore, love is greater than faith and hope because it is of the very nature and character of God Himself.

(2) *Love is greater than faith and hope because without God's love we would have no faith or hope.* Faith and hope in our hearts are put there by the love of God. It is God's love that is the ground upon which faith and hope are built. They in turn direct our hearts to love God Who first loved us (I John 4:19). ". . . God so loved the world that He gave . . ." That's where it starts. Jesus Christ came because of the Father's love. I John 4:9 says, "By this the love of God was manifested in us, that God has sent His only begotten Son into the world so that we might live through Him." Jesus died on the cross for our sins because of His great love. Romans 5:8 says, "But God demonstrates His own love toward us, in that while we were yet sinners, Christ died for us." I John 3:16 adds, "We know love by this, that He laid down His life for us . . ." We are saved because of God's

great love. Ephesians 2:4 says, "But God, being rich in mercy, because of His great love with which He loved us." Verses 5-10 of that same chapter go on to describe the wonderful salvation we have because of the one fact that God loved us. Praise the Lord! Without God's *LOVE*, there would be no faith and hope!

(3) *Love is greater than faith and hope because of its wider application.* Faith and hope are both directed toward God alone. Love is not only directed to God (as the first priority), but also to ourselves and others, both believers and non-believers, both friends and enemies. According to the Bible, the more love we have toward God, the greater will be the love we have toward others. The entire book of I John makes this crystal clear. In I John 3:17-18, we read:

> "But whoever has the world's goods, and beholds his brother in need and closes his heart against him, how does the love of God abide in him? Little children, let us not love with word or with tongue, but in deed and truth."

I John 4:11 says, "Beloved, if God so loved us, we also ought to love one another." I John 4:20-21 adds:

> "If some one says, 'I love God,' and hates his brother, he is a liar; for the one who does not love his brother whom he has seen, cannot love God whom he has not seen. And this commandment we have from Him, that the one who loves God should love his brother also."

I John 5:1 says, ". . . whoever loves the Father loves the child born of Him." God's *LOVE* is greater than faith and hope because of its wider application.

(4) *Love is greater than faith and hope because it is the primary motive for obedience and service.* Paul said it in II Corinthians 5:14, "For the love of Christ controls us . . ." The King James Version uses the word "constrains." Christ's *LOVE* for us is the driving force behind all Christian commitment. Jesus said in John 14:15, "If you love Me, you will keep my commandments." God's *LOVE* is not controlling a disobedient life. When we decide to violate God's commands, we indicate our lack of love for God. I John 5:2-3 describes this:

> "By this we know that we love the children of God, when we love God and observe His commandments. For this is the love of God, that we keep His commandments; and His commandments are not burdensome."

If you love God, you will obey Him. That principle is evident in our homes and families. The natural response of our children is to disobey. Rules and regulations that we impose upon them do not remove the desire to disobey, they only heighten and intensify that desire. Paul spoke of that in Romans 7:8-9:

> "But sin, taking opportunity through the commandment, produced in me coveting of every kind; for apart from the Law sin is dead. And I was once alive apart from the Law; but when the commandment came, sin became alive, and I died."

Paul said in I Timothy 1:9, "realizing the fact that law is not made for a righteous man, but for those who are lawless and rebellious, . . ." Obedience to God's commands cannot be controlled by man or his laws. The motivation to obey arises out of God's love. Loving God produces a submitting heart, a willingness to obey. It is hard to admit at times that the reason we do not obey God is because we do not love God!

(5) *Love is greater than faith and hope because love is that which edifies other believers.* Ephesians 4:15 says we are to be "speaking the truth in love," and the result of this will be "the growth of the body for the building up of itself in love (v. 16)." I Corinthians 8:1 says, "love edifies." I need to grow in my faith and my hope in the Lord. That benefits me, and perhaps indirectly affects others. But that which builds other believers up is love! Colossians 3:14 says, "And beyond all these things put on love, which is the perfect bond of unity." Believers experience the closeness of their unity through application of God's love. Galatians 5:13 says, ". . . through love serve one another."

(6) *Love is greater than faith and hope because love can do what faith and hope cannot do.* Faith does not forgive, and neither does hope. But love does. Ephesians

4:32-5:2 tells us to forgive one another, and that this is possible if we learn to walk in love as Christ has loved us. Colossians 3:12-14 tells us the same truth that forgiveness is rooted in the love and compassion of the Lord. It is the love of Christ that has forgiven us our sins. We deserve judgment and Hell. Thank God that He loves us! I Peter 4:8 puts it beautifully when it says, ''Above all, keep fervent in your love for one another, because love covers a multitude of sins.''

A marriage cannot be what God wants it to be without God's *LOVE* continually forgiving each other. There have been so many times when I have failed to live up to the expectations of my wife and others. I have disappointed her both in what I have done and what I have not done. Thank God she is a loving and forgiving partner! Without forgiveness, our marriage could not survive!

(7) *Love is greater than faith and hope because it does not depend upon things outside of itself in order to function.* Faith requires an object to be trusted. Romans 10:17 says, ''So faith comes from hearing, and hearing by the word of Christ.'' Our faith does not save us - Christ saves us! Our faith rests upon the facts about Christ that are found in the Bible.

Hope is based on promises. God promises things to us that we have yet to experience. Romans 8:24-25 tells us about the importance of hope. It says, ''For in hope we have been saved, but hope that is seen is not hope; for why does one also hope for what he sees? But if we hope for what we do not see, with perseverance we wait eagerly for it.'' Our hope is not ''whistling in the dark,'' but it is rather ''an anchor of the soul, a hope both sure and steadfast (Hebrews 6:19).'' The reason for this is the character of God Himself. Hebrews 6:18 says, ''. . . it is impossible for God to lie, . . .'' What God promises, He performs. Our hope is strong because of Who God is.

Love, in contrast to faith and hope, does not require a response or a reason in order to exist and function. Human love demands a response. ''If you love me, then I'll love you" - that's the world's view. God's *LOVE* is much different. Even when people do not respond and are quite antagonistic to you, you can still love them with God's *LOVE*. Love is greater than faith and hope in this regard. Love works toward others when there is no reason or response. That's the nature of God's *LOVE* - it continues to give and give, without thought of what it receives. The joy of giving dominates the one who knows God's *LOVE*. The world says "grab all the gusto you can get!" It continually reminds us to "get it while you can." That's not the way God's *LOVE* responds. It gives!

Today I had the joy of sharing with a friend that God's *LOVE* is really the greatest thing of all, and definitely the greatest need in his life. He and his wife are going through some difficult times. His wife is very discouraged and withdrawing from others. She wonders about God's *LOVE* for her because of things that have happened in her life. They are both Christians. He has constantly referred to her problems, seeking help for her. Today I was able to share with him in a special way. He really wanted help - that's where it usually starts - you must want help. I told him that the reason why his wife was insecure and discouraged was his problem, not hers. She needs a husband who will love her for what she is. He needs to stop expecting things of her. He is very demanding without realizing it. He wants her to change, and is not accepting her like she is. He is self-centered in his goals and interests. He did not understand that love surpasses knowledge, and that knowledge makes you arrogant, but love edifies. He, like many of us, seeks for knowledge about God without seeking God Himself. He needs to be broken inside and humbled before God . He needs to seek the Lord and His *LOVE* in his life as the most important goal. When he starts loving his wife with God's *LOVE*, she will become more secure and will find her needs being met.

This story is repeated over and over in the lives of people. The greatest need we all have (once we have become believers in Jesus Christ) is to be controlled by God's great

LOVE! His *LOVE* is truly the greatest! The Holy Spirit of God produces that love in the heart of the Spirit-filled believer. Knowing about love is important, but when it's working in your life, it surpasses knowledge (Ephesians 3:19).

Pursue
Love
IT'S YOUR GREATEST NEED
FIRST CORINTHIANS 13

APPLICATION

PRIORITIES IN LOVING

RELATIONSHIPS THAT SHOW LOVE

9 | Priorities in loving

The application of God's *LOVE* in our lives is where we have difficulty. We should learn about God's *LOVE*, and I Corinthians 13 is the best place to acquire that knowledge. But, it can't stop with knowing about it - we have to apply it.

This study has convinced me that simply knowing about God's *LOVE* is not enough. I have spent hours studying this subject, but that does not mean I am experiencing it. I was keenly aware of that the other night as I was sharing with my wife about what I was learning, and at the same time getting upset by her lack of response to my great revelations! I felt the Spirit of God's convicting power as I realized my failure to love my wife when she did not respond. After all, that's what I had learned about God's *LOVE* (Or, had I?)!

My wife often spells "love" with the word "time." She interprets my love in terms of the amount of time I spend with her. Time is a matter of priorities. We usually give time to that which is important to us. Sometimes it is embarrassing to take a good long look at how we spend our time. We waste much of it, and yet, in a certain sense, we are doing what we want to do with it. Priorities affect us more than we realize. Our priorities are not always right, but when it's important to us, we usually take the time to do it.

There are certain priorities in this matter of God's *LOVE*. Once we have become Christians and have experienced the *LOVE* of God for us, love toward God, ourselves, and others falls into certain definite priorities as we attempt to live our lives with His *LOVE* controlling all we do.

We're to love God first above anything and everyone.

The root as to why many people do not experience God's *LOVE* in their lives and in their relationships with other people, is found in their failure to love God first. Jesus said in Matthew 22:37-38:

> "You shall love the Lord your God with all your heart, and with all your soul, and with all your mind. This is the great and foremost commandment."

This reply was in answer to a lawyer's question, "Which is the great commandment in the Law?" The words come from Deuteronomy 6:5: "And you shall love the Lord your God with all your heart and with all your soul and with all your might." This was said to the parents as they prepared to teach their children the words and ways of the Lord. It all begins by the parents loving God first and wholeheartedly.

To an orthodox church in Ephesus came this message from Christ through the Apostle John (Revelation 2:4): "But I have this against you, that you have left your first love." The only solution was to repent (verse 5). It doesn't mean merely to cry and feel sorry for what you have done. It means to change your mind and conduct.

But how will we know if we are loving God first and wholeheartedly? I John 5:3 says, "For this is the love of God, that we keep His commandments; . . ." John 14:15 gives us Christ's words: "If you love Me, you will keep My commandments." The test of our love for God is our obedience to Him.

Ask yourself this question: "Is there any habit of mine that I am currently doing that violates a known principle or teaching of God's Word?" Make a list. Until you stop, you cannot say you love God first and wholeheartedly. Or, try this question: "Is there something which God's Word teaches you that you are neglecting or refusing to do?" James 4:17 says, "Therefore, to one who knows the right thing to do, and does not do it, to him it is sin." If we love

God first, then we will obey Him. I John 5:3 reminds us that "...His commandments are not burdensome." The commandments of Christ are not a heavy load at all. It is the devil's lie that says the commandments of Christ are too heavy a load for us to bear. They do not weigh us down - they give us relief and rest! Jesus said in Matthew 11:28-30:

> "Come to Me, all who are weary and heavy-laden, and I will give you rest. Take My yoke upon you, and learn from Me, for I am gentle and humble in heart; and you shall find rest for your soul. For My yoke is easy, and My load is light."

Coming under the yoke of Christ will bring rest and peace to our souls! Obedience to God brings blessing to the believer! It brings relief and rest! How foolish we are not to love God first and wholeheartedly. Jesus indicated the seriousness of this in Matthew 10:37 when He said, "He who loves father or mother more than Me is not worthy of Me; and he who loves son or daughter more than Me is not worthy of Me." No one comes before the Lord! He is number one!

We're to love ourselves because God loves us.

This is a difficult point, but a most important one. Some will misinterpret. Loving yourself can be very selfish and the very reason why we don't experience God's *LOVE* in our hearts toward others. On the other hand, the Bible indicates that we are to love ourselves if we hope to love others. When Jesus said in Matthew 22:37-38 that we are to love God first and that this is the greatest commandment of all, He also said that a second commandment was like this first commandment. In verse 39 He said, "And a second is like it, you shall love your neighbor as yourself."

The phrase "love your neighbor *as yourself*" indicates the necessity of self-love in our list of priorities. The words come from Leviticus 19:18. The key to interpreting this phrase "as yourself" is found, I believe, in the opening words of Matthew 22:39 when Jesus said, "And a second is like it, ..." He meant that to "...love your neighbor as yourself" was like loving God first and wholeheartedly. The two are like each other, and the first controls the second. Loving

God first and wholeheartedly causes me to love myself. This is not selfish and destructive, but a healthy kind of love and self-esteem. The "self" I am to love is not merely the outward appearance (which man always emphasizes - cf. I Samuel 16:7), but the man God sees. God sees worth and value in my life, otherwise He would not have saved me. As to my sinful, unregenerated nature, I am nothing and worthless before God. My righteousness is like filthy rags in his sight, my heart deceitful and desperately wicked. But, thanks to His love and redemption, I have been made a child of God with outstanding privileges and possessions! I am worth something to God - praise the Lord! He loves me no matter what I do or say (which He always knows quite well!). He accepts me on the basis of His love and grace, not my performance or personal worthiness - praise God!

Yes, you must love yourself. Until you do, you will not love others as God does. You must love yourself the way God loves you - with total forgiveness and acceptance. What wonderful security and assurance is found in the arms of God's *LOVE*! Our ability to love others is directly related to our love for what God loves - namely, ourselves! If you hate yourself, there's little chance for you to love others. You may want others to love you, but it won't happen until your relationship to God changes!

If you do not forgive yourself or accept yourself as God does, you will have great difficulty in loving others and receiving love from them. There may be reasons for your inability to forgive and to accept yourself based on real guilt (which means you're guilty!) If there is specific sin in your life that you are refusing to deal with, then obviously you will have difficulty in forgiving yourself. God does not overlook your habit of sinning, either. Repentance (change of mind and conduct) is a necessary ingredient for a clear conscience and a heart that is ready to love and be loved.

There are also people who have "false guilt" and have difficulty forgiving and forgetting the past, even though the sin has been dealt with, and the blood of Jesus Christ has cleansed them. The problem here is doubt and unbelief.

You begin to question whether God has forgiven you or not. You sometimes interpret difficult experiences and hard times as an indication that God does not love you, or that He hasn't really forgiven you after all. You have a tendency to forget the teaching of Hebrews 12:6, "For those whom the Lord loves He disciplines . . ."

Many years ago I counselled a lady who was on a course of hating herself and doubting God's love and forgiveness. She tried to take her life several times and did all kinds of things to make her husband and her family hate her. She was miserable and unhappy. She found herself hating God as well. It took quite a long time for her to get back to the teaching of God's Word, but when she finally did, she once again discovered the great truths of God's sovereignty and love for her. She began to accept God's love and forgiveness, and her love for herself began to grow. She started to dress more nicely, and to fix her hair in an attractive manner. She began to love her husband and her children again. We were all thrilled.

You must love yourself as God loves you. Only then can you begin to love others as God wants. Everything is rooted in your love for God. It must come first, because loving others as well as loving yourself is based on it!

We're to love our marital partner more than others.

The tragedies of today's marriages remind us of this important priority. Our love for others is not more important than our husbands or wives. Your marital partner comes first. It is based on a commitment you have made, a vow you have spoken. You have chosen to be faithful to this one person until death parts you. You have willingly set others aside for the benefit of your marital partner. You are committed to love him or her in a special way, more intimate than any other relationship in your life (outside of your love for the Lord).

Ephesians 5:25 tells husbands to ". . . love your wives, just as Christ also loved the church and gave Himself up for her." What a standard His *LOVE* is! In verse 28 it says, "So husbands ought also to love their own wives as their own bodies. He who loves his own wife loves himself.'' This reminds us that we are to love ourselves, but it also tells us to bring our marriage partners into such close intimacy and relationship with ourselves that we treat them with equal value and honor as ourselves.

Proverbs 5:18-20 speaks of this intimate marital love:

"Let your fountain be blessed, and rejoice in the wife of your youth. As a loving hind and a graceful doe, let her breasts satisfy you at all times; be exhilarated always with her love. For why should you, my son, be exhilarated with an adulteress, and embrace the bosom of a foreigner?"

It is not wrong for a husband to say to his wife, "I love you more than anyone else on earth!" That's the way it should be! Next to our Lord and our love for ourselves, flows our love for our marital partners. The security which a wife experiences is related to the special love she enjoys from her husband. Song of Solomon 2:4 ways, ". . . And his banner over me is love." The wife says of her husband in Song of Solomon 5:10, "My beloved is dazzling and ruddy, outstanding among ten thousand." Yes, the Bible teaches that love for your husband or wife should be special. It is more important than any other relationship outside of your commitment to Christ. We are to forsake all others, and to cleave to our marital partners.

In conversation with a couple one day, I discovered they were having a disagreement over the husband's involvement in other people's lives. The wife was jealous of her husband's time, and questioning his love for her. They were both Christians and planning to go into full-time service for the Lord. The husband felt that his wife was not as committed to the Lord as she should be. The wife felt that the husband was not committed to her as he should be. What do you do in a situation like that? Here's what I did. I called the husband over to the other side of the room where we were to have a private little talk. I said, "Who do you think is responsible in this situation?" He wasn't sure. I said, "You are. You are the spiritual leader, the husband of this home. You are to cleave or glue yourself to your wife. I want to ask you a personal question, may I?'' He said, ''OK.'' I said, ''Is your wife the most important person to you next to Jesus?'' He got the point real fast, and thanked me. I suggested to him that he show her just how important of a priority she was in his life by spending a special time each week with her. He said he wasn't sure if he could do that. I told him that until an appointment with his wife each week was a priority, she would probably continue to question his loyalty and love. He responded by establishing a weekly date with her. He has often told me how much he appreciated that advice through the years since.

We are not free to love others until we have clearly established the priority of our marital partner. Next to the Lord, your marital partner is the most important person on earth to you! Never forget that and you will save yourself much heartache and pain!

We're to love our children above others.

They can give you a rough time and frequently disappoint you, but they belong to you, and you are responsible. You are to love them. Titus 2:4 emphasizes this priority when it says to young mothers, ''... to love their husbands (1st priority), to love their children (2nd priority).'' I Timothy 5:8 puts a special emphasis on this when it says, ''But if any one does not provide for his own, and *especially* for those of his household, he has denied the faith, and is worse than an unbeliever.'' Pretty strong language, don't you think? Evidently God considers neglect of your family a very serious matter.

It is tragic the way children are ignored and neglected by their parents. Many children are raised by their grandparents. They have divorced parents, and learn early to fend for themselves. That sign on the back of cars that says, ''Have you hugged your kid today?'' is a tremendous truth!

We're to love other believers.

Jesus said in John 13:34-35:

''A new commandment I give to you, that you love one another, even as I have loved you, that you also love one another. By this all men will know that you are My disciples, if you have love for one another.''

The Apostle John is so strong on this point that he writes in I John 2:9, "The one who says he is in the light and yet hates his brother is in the darkness until now." In verse 11, he adds, "But the one who hates his brother is in the darkness and walks in the darkness, and does not know where he is going because the darkness has blinded his eyes." Love for our brothers and sisters in Christ is a mark of salvation. The absence of such love as a pattern of life is evidence of one who has never been born again.

The reason why we do not love our brothers and sisters (if that is true) is found in I John 3:11-12:

> "For this is the message which you have heard from the beginning, that we should love one another; not as Cain, who was of the evil one, and slew his brother. And for what reason did he slay him? Because his deeds were evil, and his brother's were righteous."

Evil deeds are behind the lack of loving one's brother. Sinful patterns and practices in our lives will hinder the flow of God's love. Continued sinning is a clear indication that we have never been saved. We can make all the excuses we want, and spend much time defending ourselves, but if we can continue to sin without repentance and conviction, it is a sure sign that we have never been born again!

Loving one's brother means that we respond to needs. I John 3:17-18 says:

> "But whoever has the world's goods, and beholds his brother in need and closes his heart against him, how does the love of God abide in him? Little children, let us not love with word or with tongue, but in deed and truth."

When the Bible uses the word "brother" it is normally talking about another believer. According to the Bible, believers have a special responsibility to other believers that they do not have toward the world of unbelievers. When our efforts to reach our world for Christ involve hurting fellow brothers and sisters in Christ, we have the wrong methods and practice. It is our love for one another that attracts the unbeliever to Christ.

Loving other believers is not an option, but a command.

I John 4:7 says, "Beloved, let us love one another, for love is from God; and every one who loves is born of God and knows God." In verse 11, we read, "Beloved, if God so loved us, we also ought to love one another." In verse 21 it says, "And this commandment we have from him, that the one who loves God should love his brother also."

One day a friend was telling me of all he was doing to share his faith in Christ. He had the latest methods, and what he felt was the "right approach." He spent many hours at it, and he seemed proud of his accomplishments. I was struck by the absence of love for other believers in what he said. He was caustic and critical of believers, often putting them down for not doing things the way he was doing them. I confronted him with the words of the Bible about love for one another. He didn't respond. I felt sorry for him. Today he does not have an effective ministry. He still has problems in loving other believers. Little does he realize that loving other believers would enhance his witness to unbelievers. When they see our love for one another, then they will become convinced that we are the disciples of Jesus Christ!

We're to love the world of non-believers.

Galatians 6:10 says, "So then, while we have opportunity, let us do good to all men, and *especially* to those who are of the household of the faith." Yes, we have a special relationship with believers that we do not have with the world. But, we are to "do good" to the world as well. John 3:16 says, "For God so loved the world . . ." I Timothy 4:10 states that our hope is in the living God ". . . Who is the Savior of all men, *especially* of believers." Christ died for the "whole world" according to I John 2:2. He is the "propitiation for our sins; and not for ours only, but also for those of the whole world." The word "propitiation" refers to the mercy-seat of the tabernacle where the high priest placed the blood once a year on the Day of Atonement as a satisfaction of the righteous wrath of God against sin. The individual Jew who did not bring his individual sacrifices for his sins was cut off from the Messianic hope, and yet, in some sense, the entire nation was atoned for on the Day of Atonement. God's wrath against the sin of all men was satisfied by the blood put on the mercy seat on the Day of Atonement. Propitiation has been done for the whole world. But only those who show their personal faith in the blood sacrifice by bringing their individual sacrifices for sin would be redeemed. Believers are redeemed, unbelievers are not. All people have the opportunity for redemption because of the propitiation (satisfaction) of Christ's death on the cross, but all will not be saved. To put it another way: Christ's death was sufficient for the whole world in terms of payment for sin; but it was efficient and is efficient only for those who believe. It's no good for you until you believe in the Lord Jesus Christ as your personal Saviour from sin, death, and Hell!

If God's *LOVE* encompasses the whole world, should not we love the world of unbelievers? If His *LOVE* dwells in our hearts, then we must love the world.

Jesus revealed His love for the world when he saw the multitudes. Matthew 9:36 says, ''. . . He felt compassion for them, because they were distressed and downcast like sheep without a shepherd.'' That compassion of Christ was seen in Luke 19:41 when it says of Jesus as he approached the city of Jerusalem that would reject Him: ''. . . He saw the city and wept over it.''

The Apostle Paul reveals his heart of love for the unbelieving when he wrote in Romans 9:1-3:

> ''I am telling the truth in Christ, I am not lying, my conscience bearing me witness in the Holy Spirit, that I have great sorrow and unceasing grief in my heart. For I could wish that I myself were accursed, separated from Christ for the sake of my brethren, my kinsmen according to the flesh.''

In Romans 10:1 he said, ''Brethren, my heart's desire and my prayer to God for them is for their salvation.''

This love for the lost flows from Christ's love for us. II Corinthians 5:14 says, ''For the love of Christ controls us . . .'', and then in verse 20 of that same chapter it says, ''Therefore, we are ambassadors for Christ, as though God were entreating through us; we beg you on behalf of Christ, be reconciled to God.'' Only Christ can give you a heart of compassion and love for the world of unbelievers, so that your one main goal and desire is that they might be saved. Paul wrote in I Corinthians 9:22, ''. . . I have become all things to all men, that I may by all means save some.''

Summary on Priorities

God's *LOVE* is based on infinite resources. You will never know the depths of His *LOVE*. There is always more available than you have ever experienced or known. God's *LOVE* controlling our hearts, can make us able and available to meet all these priorities. Take a look at them again and remember that each of them involves time, energy, and resources.

1. We are to love God first above anything and everyone.
2. We are to love ourselves because God loves us.
3. We are to love our marital partner more than others.
4. We are to love our children above others.
5. We are to love other believers.
6. We are to love the world of non-believers.

Make a list of things you intend to do to demonstrate these priorities in loving. Be sure to indicate when you will do them. The ''when'' is just as important as the ''what.'' It takes time to love, but it is time well spent, doing the greatest thing of all - loving! Love is really the greatest!

Relationships that show love | 10

It is one thing to say we ought to love one another; it's quite another thing to show it! Sixteen times in the New Testament we are told to "love one another." On two of those occasions we are exhorted to love one another "fervently (I Peter 1:22 and 4:8)." The word "fervent" or "fervently" comes from a root word meaning "to stretch" and a preposition meaning "out." "To stretch out" indicates an intense, or strenuous effort. To love one another the way God wants us to, takes some hard work!

What does it mean to "love one another?" The word translated "one another (allelon - Greek)" is used about 100 times in the New Testament, including 40 usages by the Apostle Paul. Our relationships as believers are revealed in the many usages of "one another." They all manifest the practical qualities of our basic responsibility, that of "loving one another." They help us to identify the meaning of love among believers, and to make practical applications in our daily lives.

To love one another involves complete acceptance of other believers.

Romans 15:7 says, "Wherefore, accept one another, just as Christ also accepted us to the glory of God." This passage in its context (cf. Romans 14) deals with our attitudes toward other believers when they differ with us over non-essentials like the kind of food we eat, or the importance of certain days. Romans 14:1 states, "Now accept the one who is weak in faith, but not for the purpose of passing judgment on his opinions.''

Learning to accept each other when there are minor disagreements is a quality of God's *LOVE*. If we can't agree to disagree on non-essentials, we will not get far in our attempts to love others. Some things are worth fighting for, and dying for, but other things, you can take or leave. Good Bible teachers disagree frequently on the interpretation of various passages in the Bible. It is foolish for any one of us to think that we have the ultimate truth on any given passage! We do our best, but there are times when we must be gracious and kind toward those who disagree with us.

Romans 12:5 says, "So we, who are many, are one body in Christ, and individually members one of another.'' The teaching of the body with its many members appears frequently in Paul's writings, and a rather lengthy discussion on it is found in I Corinthians 12. Each member as a part of the overall body has a spiritual gift to use in building up other members of the body. We must learn to accept the ministries of others, even though they be quite different from our own. We do not all have the same gifts. There is diversity in the body. The eye cannot say to the hand, "I don't need you." We are all needed. We are "members one of another."

I John 1:7 tells us that all believers have "fellowship with one another." The word "fellowship" refers to that which we share in common. Although used in a variety of ways in the New Testament, the context of I John 1 reveals that the "fellowship" we have is the fact we all share eternal life, God's life within us. That which makes us one is the life of God within each believer. Many of us do not enjoy the fellowship we already have. We have not learned to accept other believers. If they have come to know Jesus Christ as Lord and Saviour, then we are one with them in the body of Christ - we have fellowship with them.

Some of the problems that I have observed in Christians accepting one another may seem to some people to be ridiculous, but to others, they are real problems. Take a moment and reflect on these problems as possible hindrances to our acceptance of other believers: (1) Racial differences, (2) Economic differences, (3) Job level differences, (4) Charismatic differences, (5) Musical taste differences, (6) Style of dress differences, (7) Methods of ministry differences, (8) Age differences. No doubt you could add to the list! Some times churches tolerate these differences in their midst, but there never is full, complete acceptance. Let's face it - we are all different in our backgrounds, cultural preferences, dress styles, tastes, methods, etc. We must learn to love each other with complete acceptance, and stop judging each other.

To love one another involves physical affection toward other believers.

Romans 16:16 says, "Greet one another with a *holy* kiss. All the churches of Christ greet you." (cf. I Corinthians 16:20 and II Corinthians 13:12). In I Thessalonians 5:26 we read, "Greet *all* the brethren with a holy kiss." I Peter 5:14 adds, "Greet one another with a kiss *of love*." The word "kiss" comes from the Greek word for love which refers to the love of friends. It is not an erotic or sensual kiss. It is the kiss of friends.

It is used of Judas kissing our Lord Jesus Christ, a kiss of betrayal. It is used in Luke 7:45 when Jesus pointed out to Simon the Pharisee that he had not given him the common greeting of a kiss, but the woman had repeatedly kissed his feet. In its verb form, it is used in Luke 15:20 of the father who fell on the neck of his prodigal son, and repeatedly kissed him. It is used in Acts 20:37 when Paul and the Ephesian elders embraced and they repeatedly kissed him. It is used five times in the epistles where believers are exhorted to greet one another.

Some argue that the kiss of greeting among believers is simply a common custom. That seems to be the implication of Luke 7:45 as it relates to Simon the Pharisee. It might also explain the greeting of Judas when he betrayed Christ. Depending upon the cultural acceptance, this greeting should simply conform to the standard greeting among all people (according to this view). If it is common to shake hands, then the greeting would simply be a handshake. If it is common to embrace, then the greeting would conform to that. If a kiss is acceptable, then the kiss would be used. The problem of men with men, women with women, or men with women, would depend upon the particular culture involved.

There are others, however, who believe that such cultural interpretation does not fully explain the close relationship which the believers enjoyed and treasured. In each of the five "greeting" passages, the exhortation is directed only to believers. If it is a common greeting for all, why would there not be exhortation to greet all, both believers as well as unbelievers? Also, the scene of Paul and the Ephesian elders in Acts 20 is not easily explained by cultural practice. There was embracing and repeated kissing in that context. There was sorrow in their hearts over the possibility that they would never see Paul again in this life. The woman of Luke 7:45 cannot be dismissed by reference to cultural practice. She was kissing the feet of Jesus, an obvious distasteful act to Simon the Pharisee. Her kiss was one of love for Jesus, not a common greeting.

While Christians seem to disagree over the interpretation of this greeting, it is interesting to note that it is a command in the Greek. It is not a suggestion based on personal convenience or cultural preference, but a command. In all five usages of this kiss of greeting, the tense of the verb "greet" is aorist, which indicates a moment of time, not a continuous action. There is no suggestion of any sexual connotation, either in the tense of the verb or in the word used for "kiss" - which is based on the Greek word for the love of friends, not erotic or sensual love.

In these five passages dealing with the kiss of greeting, there are two important qualifications on this practice. First, *All* the believers were to be greeted with a kiss - I Thessalonians 5:26. There would certainly be some question about a believer who chose to kiss only one or two people in a group of many believers. While the size of the crowd would certainly be a factor, the normal situation which the average believer faces usually involves just a few people. If you have some believers into your home for fellowship, and you want to apply this kiss of greeting, be sure to kiss each one, not just your favorite few!

Secondly, The greeting is to be a *holy* kiss. That adjective "holy" suggests the possiblity of a kiss being "unholy." The word "holy" is a reminder of the dangers of the flesh, and the constant temptation to use this warm and loving greeting among believers for selfish and sensual purposes.

In some societies, men kissing men is appropriate, while in others, it suggests immorality and poor taste at best. Christians need to be aware of such situations and feelings. If God's *LOVE* is controlling our hearts, we will not do anything to offend or to turn fellow believers away from the Lord. Men kissing women is natural in the process of marital love, but one can easily see the dangers of such practice among believers who are not married. Unless there is a "holy" kiss, much suspicion, jealousy, and emotional hurt can result.

In all of this discussion, do not miss the main point. If we love each other, there will be affection shown. It is to be controlled, and done without partiality. Some people will be hesitant to show or receive such physical affection. Perhaps they have deep feelings about it that are rooted in bitter experiences of the past. Loving Christians need to be sensitive about these problems, and respond to people as God would desire. Many people are insecure and become quite nervous over any show of affection. Some believers are content not to pursue such affection, preferring to "keep their distance" or to "remain aloof." There are all kinds of problems to be faced, but love is willing to risk and to give when there is little or no response from others.

My wife and I were in a believer's home recently along with other believers. The hostess was greeting all of us with a brief embrace and kiss on the cheek. It was an enjoyable evening, and as we all left, the embrace and kiss was there to greet us. However, one of the men in the group was left out, certainly not intentionally. But, it deeply affected him. He spoke to his wife about it, and later shared it with us. It reminded us of the importance of that word "all" in the phrase, "greet *all* the brethren with a holy kiss." He began to feel that there was a wrong motive behind his being left out of that greeting. He thought he was being "left out in the cold." He wondered what he had done to offend them. We reassured him that such was not the case. We all learned a lesson from it that will help us in other situations.

To love one another involves positive attitudes toward other believers.

Galatians 5:15 and 26 remind us of attitudes we must avoid if we are to love one another the way God wants us to do. Such things as "bite, devour, challenge, envy" have no part in the love we should show to each other. We are told not to lie to one another in Colossians 3:9, and not to speak against one another in James 4:11. Our attitude toward each other is a very important matter. Consider the following five attitudes and ask yourself before God whether these characterize your relationships with other believers.

First is *Humility*. I Peter 5:5 tells us to ". . . clothe yourselves with humility toward one another . . ." Philippians 2:3 says, ". . . with humility of mind let each of you regard one another as more important than himself." When you show that kind of attitude toward other brothers and sisters in Christ, they will know you sincerely love them. Treat them as important, more important than yourself. Be concerned about the things that are of interest to them, not simply to yourself. Ephesians 5:21 emphasizes that we are to "be subject to one another." It then goes on to describe all of the relationships in life that are affected by this submission: husbands and wives, children and parents, slaves and masters.

Humility to me is listening to an elderly lady tell me something about my appearance that needed to be changed. Humility and submission is accepting the advice and counsel of others when it is different from your own opinions and viewpoints. Humility is allowing others to speak before yourself. Humility is playing a game with your children that they like, but you don't. Humility is praising others rather than yourself.

Second is *Honor*. Romans 12:10 says, ". . . give preference to one another in honor." Romans 13:7 says to give ". . . honor to whom honor" is due. Christians who love each other have a tendency to honor each other. The opposite is to tear down. Love honors others, and seeks ways to build them up, not bring them down.

Husbands are to love their wives with honor. I Peter 3:7 says, ". . . likewise, live with your wives in an understanding way, as with a weaker vessel, since she is a woman; and grant her honor as a fellow-heir of the grace of life, so that your prayers may not be hindered." When I hear husbands speak of their wives as "the old lady," and describe the failures and weaknesses of their wives, I get disturbed. That is not loving, and it will ultimately hurt their relationship with their wives.

Third is *Loyalty*. Romans 12:10 says, "Be devoted to one another in brotherly love; . . ." That emphasizes family ties. As believers, we are in the same family. There ought to be family loyalty and devotion to one another. We ought to protect and defend each other. I Peter 4:8 says, "love covers a multitide of sins."

I liked it when I heard a dear lady say of a Christian friend who had supposedly fallen into sin, "Well, I just can't believe that of him. As a matter of fact, I won't believe it until I hear it from his own lips." She was loyal to another brother in Christ. They were family, and it showed.

Fourth is *Care*. I Corinthians 12:25-26 says:

"That there should be no division in the body, but that the members should have the same care for one another. And if one member suffers, all the members suffer with it; if one member is honored, all the members rejoice with it."

That's the way it should be when God's *LOVE* is controlling our attitudes. Caring for each other implies a deep identification with the needs of others. When we hear of needs among our fellow believers, love must respond. It cannot sit idly by and do nothing!

One of the men in our church who became ill with cancer was overwhelmed by the love shown to him by other believers. He could hardly believe how people offered to help and minister to him in time of need. God used that experience to show him His *LOVE* in a special way that has since meant so much to his Christian life. "If one member suffers, all the members suffer with it."

The last one is *Forbearance.* Ephesians 4:2 says, ". . . showing forbearance to one another in love." "Forbearance" means "to put up" with one another. It means we will endure at times the faults and weaknesses of our brothers and sisters. Colossians 3:13 makes it a necessary ingredient in the matter of forgiveness: "Bearing with one another, and forgiving each other, whoever has a complaint against any one; just as the Lord forgave you, so also should you."

It is difficult to forgive some one when you know the problem still exists. We must learn to forgive even when the people we are forgiving probably will not change their habits or practices. Many of us put a condition on our forgiveness that demands that people change. But, life is not like that - people have a tendency to remain the same - have you noticed?

I was discussing a marital problem with a certain couple a few years ago, when I realized the problem of forgiving someone when you know things will not change. This wife was having a difficult time adjusting to a husband who did many things that irritated her. She was accustomed to rolling up the end of the toothpaste and pushing the remainder of the toothpaste to the top. He always pushed it in the middle and failed to roll it up neatly. This irritated her. She liked him to hang up his clothes the moment he took them off, but his constant habit was to throw them in a chair. It was driving her crazy! She knew that she should forgive him, but what was bothering her was that she knew he would not change his habits. What should she do? That's what "forbearance" is all about. When you love someone, you learn to put up with differences. You stop trying to change them, and instead, learn to accept them and love them as they are.

Attitudes are important. God's *LOVE* responds with humility, honor, loyalty, care, and forbearance. These "one another" relationships show us much about what it means to "love one another."

To love one another involves specific actions that help other believers.

These "actions" are based on proper "attitudes." They are motivated by God's *LOVE*. They do not depend upon the worthiness of the person to whom you are ministering. Some of them are difficult to do, and often become the real test of our love for people. All of them need Divine help and direction.

The first action is *Hospitality*. The word means "loving guests or strangers." I Peter 4:9 says, "Be hospitable to one another without complaint." Many believers complain about the obligation and duty of having other believers into their home. That's not love - that's obligation! Is your home (and life) open to others? Do you love to have people in your home for times of fellowship? It is a mark of Christian love. It is a specific action that says "I love you" to those you invite.

The second is *Prayer*. James 5:16 states, "Therefore, confess your sins to one another, and pray for one another, so that you may be healed . . ." It is love that causes us to pray for brothers and sisters in Christ who are sick and suffering. Those who do not love, usually do not pray.

Some of the sweetest words I hear people say are, "I've been praying for you." One dear Christian lady told me that I have been on her prayer list for many years, and that a day does not go by that she would fail to mention my name in prayer. You can imagine the joy in my heart to know of her faithful prayers for me! I believe she really loves me!

The third action is *Encouragement*. How we need to be encouraged! The Bible says this in so many ways. The word "comfort" is often used, and refers to one who is called alongside of another to help. It is often translated"exhort" like in II Timothy 4:2 where it says, "exhort, with great patience and instruction." Encouragement takes patience with people. I Thessalonians 5:11 says, "Therefore encourage one another, and build up one another, just as you also are doing." I Thessalonians 4:18 tells us to "comfort one another with these words (words about the coming of our Lord)."

Paul spoke of his own ministry of encouraging other believers when he wrote in I Thessalonians 2:11, "just as you know how we were exhorting and encouraging and imploring each one of you as a father would his own children." We need a father's heart to bring encouragement to others. Hebrews 10:24-25 says:

"And let us consider how to stimulate one another to love and good deeds, not forsaking our own assembling together, as is the habit of some, but encouraging one another; and all the more, as you see the day drawing near."

We need to challenge others to love and good deeds. We need to spend time assembling with other believers in order to encourage them. We all need it!

Paul spoke of how believers can encourage each other when he said in Romans 1:12, "that I may be encouraged together with you while among you, each of us by the other's faith, both yours and mine." There was mutual encouragement involved here. Paul wanted to encourage them and he in turn knew that they would encourage him. That's the way it often happens. You set out to bring encouragement to some other believer, and you wind up being encouraged all the more!

I went into a hospital room one day to give encouragement to a dying believer. Little did I realize when I walked into that room that the one who would do the most encouraging that day was that dying believer, not me! That person's hope and confidence in the Lord made a deep impression on my soul. I cannot forget it. It encourages my heart when I think about the incident. I pray that I will be the same kind of blessing to others when I am at death's door!

Don't you love to be around people who are always encouraging others? I have a good friend in the ministry who is like that. He is such a joy to be around. He is always encouraging others. It's contagious - you want to minister to others because of what he's done for you. His love is evident.

The fourth is *Admonishment* (Warning). This is one of the more difficult ministries believers are to do. But, it is a sign of love. Romans 15:14 speaks of believers who are "able to admonish one another" because they are "full of goodness, filled with all knowledge." It takes a godly lifestyle and a mature knowledge to be able effectively to confront other believers and warn them. Galatians 6:1-2 speaks of this:

> "Brethren, even if a man is caught in any trespass, you who are spiritual, restore such a one in a spirit of gentleness; each one looking to yourself, lest you too be tempted. Bear one another's burdens, and thus fulfill the law of Christ."

The "law of Christ" is the law of love. If we love one another, we will lovingly confront them when we know they are walking in sinful habits and practices. It is not love that refuses to confront other believers who are living in sin. If you really care, you do not want to see your fellow believers ruin their lives and get all messed up by sin. It is not love that says, "They'll get what they deserve."

Paul spoke of the personal struggles he had in this area when he said in Acts 20:31 to the elders of the church at Ephesus: "Therefore be on the alert, remembering that night and day for a period of three years I did not cease to admonish each one with tears." There are many tears to be shed when admonishing other believers. There must be a proper attitude when confronting others, but even when there is, it is never easy. Paul warned about a wrong attitude in I Corinthians 4:14 when he said, "I do not write these things to shame you, but to admonish you as my beloved children." We do not confront others in order to embarass them by such exposure. Love covers a multitude of sins.

Paul spoke of admonishing "with all wisdom" in Colossians 1:28 and 3:16. The goal of such admonishment is the maturity of the believer. We warn others in order to build them up, not tear them down, or shame them. Paul said in I Thessalonians 5:14 that we are to admonish the "unruly." Admonishment is a ministry that deals with confrontation. It means that we, in love, must warn fellow believers about sinful habits and practices. It is not easy to do, but it is one of the most powerful signs of true Christian love. Proverbs 27:5-6 says, "Better is open rebuke than love that is concealed. Faithful are the wounds of a friend, but deceitful are the kisses of an enemy."

The last action is *Service*. Galatians 5:13 says, "For you were called to freedom, brethren; only do not turn your freedom into an opportunity for the flesh, but through love serve one another." A servant's heart is a great barometer of Christian love. Jesus said in Mark 10:42-45:

> "You know that those who are recognized as rulers of the Gentiles lord it over them; and their great men exercise authority over them. But it is not so among you, but whoever wishes to become great among you shall be your servant; and whoever wishes to be first among you shall be slave of all. For even the Son of Man did not come to be served, but to serve, and to give His life a ransom for many."

A willingness to serve other believers is a sign of love. A "slave of all" is the one who is first with the Lord. Christ's example in this area is all we need to guide us. He, in turn, gave us much instruction in this area of service. In John 13:14-17, He said:

> "If I then, the Lord and the Teacher, washed your feet, you also ought to wash one another's feet. For I gave you an example that you also should do as I did to you. Truly, truly, I say to you, a slave is not greater than his master; neither one who is sent greater than the one who sent him. If you know these things, you are blessed if you do them."

Blessing (happiness) comes to those who "do," not simply those who "know" these things. Many of us know that we ought to serve others, but only in the doing is there the blessedness and the demonstration of love. Washing feet was a dirty and menial task. If our Lord was willing, should not we be willing also? Is there any task or service for another believer that you are unwilling to do?

A dear Christian friend called upon one of the members of our church who had been confined to his home because of illness. He had a nurse who was paid to come in and help him, but who, for one reason or another, had quit. The sick person was bedridden and needed help in every area, including urine and bowel movement. The day this friend showed up to bring some encouragement to the sick person was the day the nurse had quit, and needless to say, the man was in bad shape. The room smelled something terrible, and there was quite a mess. My Christian friend took the time to clean everything up and to care for the needs of this sick person, and even arranged for further nursing care. That's what I call "love," a willingness to serve and perform whatever task is necessary to meet the other person's needs. It was not an easy chore, but it was Christian love that responded.

Loving one another is often more practical than people realize. Instead of emotional feelings and sentimental thoughts, it is often a matter of chores and work - ministering in whatever way possible to meet the needs of fellow believers. These specific actions of hospitality, prayer, encouragement, admonishment, and service, are manifestations of our love for one another. God's *LOVE* is practical and helpful. It meets the need and doesn't avoid responsibility toward others.

God's *LOVE* is our greatest need! Nothing else will meet our need! To love and be loved - that's the highest mark of Christian maturity and growth. But, remember - it has to be God's *LOVE*, which often reflects the exact opposite of our natural human tendencies. In order to have God's *LOVE* in our lives, we need to be controlled by God's Holy Spirit! There is no substitution for a Spirit-filled life! Drop all of your excuses and defenses for not loving, and respond immediately to God's Holy Spirit! Deal with sinful attitudes and practices, for they will only hinder the precious flow of the Spirit's love in your life! Walk in obedience to what the Bible teaches, trusting God to lead and guide you in everything you do. Come to God frequently in prayer, and ask for His help - He never gets tired of your saying, "Help!" Ask Him right now to fill your life with His *LOVE*! Pursue love, for it is truly the *Greatest Need in Your Life!*